# THE WAY WE WORK

## HOW FAITH MAKES A DIFFERENCE ON THE JOB

## DAN BOONE

BEACON HILL PRESS
OF KANSAS CITY

Beacon Hill Press of Kansas City
PO Box 419527
Kansas City, MO 64141
www.beaconhillbooks.com

ISBN 978-0-8341-3247-4

Printed in the
United States of America

Cover Design: Matt Johnson
Inside Design: Sharon Page

All Scripture quotations not otherwise designated are from the *New Revised Standard Version* (NRSV) of the Bible, copyright © 1989 by the Division of Christian Education of the National Council of the Churches of Christ in the USA. All rights reserved. Used by permission.

Scripture marked TM is from *The Message* (TM). Copyright © 1993, 1994, 1995, 1996, 2000, 2001, 2002 by Eugene H. Peterson. Used by permission.

Scripture marked KJV is from the King James Version of the Bible.

The Internet addresses, email addresses, and phone numbers in this book are accurate at the time of publication. They are provided as a resource. Beacon Hill Press of Kansas City does not endorse them or vouch for their content or permanence.

**Library of Congress Cataloging-in-Publication Data**

Boone, Dan, 1952-
    The way we work : how faith makes a difference on the job / Dan Boone.
        pages cm
    Includes bibliographical references.
    ISBN 978-0-8341-3247-4 (pbk.)
    1. Work—Religious aspects—Christianity. 2. Employees—Religious life. I. Title.
    BT738.5.B67 2014
    248.8'8—dc23

                                                                2014012202

10 9 8 7 6 5 4 3 2 1

# What Others Are Saying

"I judge books by how many passages I underline, how many I highlight, and by how many passages invite me to return. This book requires a highlighter for each hand and every chapter has at least one 'I want to think on that for a while' passage. How I wish this book had been available at several passages in my work career."

—Harold Ivan Smith,
grief educator, author, and speaker

"Dan Boone's pastoral heart shines throughout this volume. Practical, winsome, and accessible, *The Way We Work* speaks with biblically informed wisdom—and hope—to everyday Christians who live in this world where our work combines both pain and pleasure. Boone truly 'gets' the common workplace dilemmas most of us face. And he responds with ancient insights in fresh prose that is made 3-D with real-life anecdotes."

—Dr. Amy L. Sherman, author
*Kingdom Calling: Vocational Stewardship for the Common Good*

"We live in a culture that persistently deceives us into believing our worth is embedded in our work and the size of our paycheck. I've read book after book on this topic as I've struggled with the tension of placing my own occupation in its proper framework. Dr. Dan Boone has managed to communicate what writers who came before him did not. *The Way We Work* is the gem of this genre. With his easy storytelling and rich conversational style, Dan has delivered a candid treatise on the necessity and context of labor in our daily lives. His words are deeply grounded in the biblical narrative and steadily remind us that God is faithfully redeeming the whole world through the dust, the sweat, and the muscle of our industriousness. Dan's writing has transformed my perspective on vocation forever. This book is a special gift for anyone longing to find the place where our work meets God's interests."

—Matt Litton, author
*Holy Nomad: The Rugged Road to Joy,*
*The Mockingbird Parables*

Dedicated to
Wayne and Eleanor Sims

Your hard work has provided for your family,
your employees,
your friends,
and the work of God in the world.
May your tribe increase.

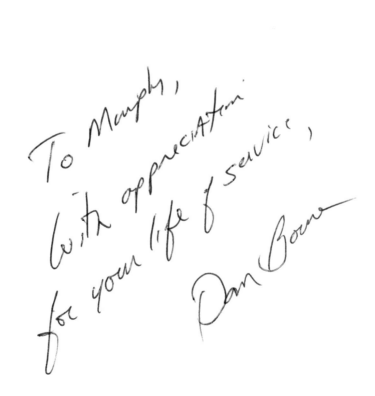

# CONTENTS

# PREFACE

## MOWING THE LAWN

I mowed my lawn this week. It was a humid, sweltering, ninety-two degrees. I have two lawn mowers—both the pushing kind, not the kind you ride on. As a person who needs more exercise, I refuse to purchase a riding lawn mower. Pushing the mower forces me to sweat, and at the completion of the weekly ritual, I experience something mysteriously sacred about the mown lawn. For all the work I do, this single ritual most acquaints me with God. I'm not sure why.

My lawn-mowing career began as a child at my grandparents' home. They had beautiful Saint Augustine grass. Even the name of it sounds holy. They owned an ancient lawn mower that had no motor. It had a twirling set of cutting blades that spun round and round, equivalent to the speed with which it was being pushed. The faster you pushed it, the better it cut. Mowing their yard was a group exercise. With twenty-seven cousins hanging around, we each pushed until we couldn't breathe, and then the next cousin took over. I cut my mowing teeth on that old mower.

Then I graduated to power mowers. At age twelve, my cousin Eddie and I started a lawn-mowing business. We were fast and dependable and cheap. And we were willing to sweat in the Mississippi summers, which were hot enough to fry eggs on sidewalks. We made good money on every yard—except one. Uncle Felix was my grandmother's brother, a widowed man who lived alone, and my dad insisted that we help Uncle Felix. He paid us ten dollars to mow his yard, but we burned up two motors cutting it. Uncle Felix was extravagance-challenged, a.k.a. cheap. He would let us mow his yard only once a month. By the time we got to it, we were practically baling hay. We mowed it about two feet at a time, pushing the tall grass down with the front of the mower, then lowering the blades into it slowly, trying not to choke the motor. It was tortuously slow work. This yard did not acquaint me with God; I almost learned to cuss, which taught me something about some kinds of work that people are required to do—a kind of work that seems distant from God and somehow estranged to God. I suppose the curse of the ground in the fall of Adam and Eve is to blame for Uncle Felix's yard.

Our business was otherwise successful. I saved more than $2,000 and paid cash for my first year of college and bought my first car. Those were the good old days. Summer of my junior year in college, Lawrence Golden and I ran a lawn-mowing business. But we had moved up in the world of grass. We had a truck and trailer, a riding mower, two push mowers, a weed whacker, and a stand-behind, self-propelled Gravely mower. We had a few residential yards, but our primary business was apartment complexes.

As partners, we hit it early in the morning and worked until late in the evening. We earned money for college, and I have always believed that my education "took" because I sweated to pay for it. One's work either fills the soul with joy or sours the heart, and what we buy with the fruit of our work reveals what we consider to be valuable.

I've always mowed my own lawn. Friends have explained to me that I earn enough to hire someone to do it, that my time is better spent doing college-president things, that I am robbing immigrants of work, that a sixty-year-old man should not work in the Tennessee heat. They could be right. They also question the sanity of my refusal to buy a riding lawn mower. I still prefer the old push mower. I did break down and buy a self-propelled mower for Denise to use. She likes yard work, and as partners, we can mow the entire lawn in ninety minutes.

Doing sacred work with someone you love is a bonding experience. In a world where a man and woman hop in bed with each other hours after meeting, I prefer the intimacy of a life-long, lawn-mowing partnership with the same woman. Again, it is sacred, because the two have become one, and they are tending God's creation—even though the sweat and toil of the curse has made it a little harder yard to mow than Eden.

Now we have a neighbor whose lawn needs mowing. She lost her husband, and her relatives are vultures; her money is running out, and she may not be able to keep her house. So we mow her lawn too. It seems to me that everybody she deals with is out to take advantage of her. She doesn't know much about car repair, air conditioning units, technology, or contracts.

I suppose some forms of work are successful only by taking advantage of people, but I wonder how these people go home and sleep at night after having cheated my neighbor. Their work is stealing hope from a woman who has already seen enough hard days. So we try to watch out for her, which also acquaints me with God and seems a sacred thing to do.

The kind of work that we are not required to do and are not compensated for may be the sweetest of all. It reminds me of God's work on our behalf. Love of neighbor is about as law-fulfilling, life-embracing as it gets. And sacred too.

So now I'll write a book about work. It is a place where divine/human encounters are played out. The tensions are remarkable. On one hand, it is a sacred partnership with God that occupies us in tending God's creation. On the other hand, it is cursed by the fall. How the same act can be gift and curse is a mystery. And our work can be done in likeness to God: creative, loving, life-embracing. Or it can be done like the devil: stealing, killing, and destroying. Work is eternal. We will be judged forever by the quality and imprint of our work. Our work follows us into tomorrow. But it is temporal. We all retire at some point, one way or another.

We are not the first people to grapple with these tensions. Work issues show up in the chronicles of the people of God. So let's visit the old texts for fresh light on the new work challenges God's people face in this postmodern world.

— 1 —

# A CHRISTIAN THEOLOGY
# OF WORK

I may have bitten off more than I can chew. To declare what the Bible says about human labor is a tall task. It would be much easier to write a theology of work from the sacred texts of country music.

There are plenty of sources to quote from. Tennessee Ernie Ford suggests that the back-breaking toil of loading sixteen tons gets you another day older and deeper in debt.[1] Dolly Parton croons that working nine to five is no way to make a living.[2] And Johnny Paycheck, a man whose last name suggests appreciation for a steady job, sings the resignation song of everyone who wants to quit: "Take this job and shove it, / I ain't workin' here no more."[3] Can I get an amen?

It appears to me that country music does not have a winsome theology of work. But are our sacred texts any better? The biblical record that says the most about work, sweat, toil, and labor is the Old Testament book of Ecclesiastes. The primary word in the book is the Hebrew word *hebel*, which is usually translated *vanity*. The word means vapor, emptiness, transitory. It is like a fog that you cannot get your fingers around. It is gone by midmorning and leaves no evidence that it was ever there. This is the word most used to describe work. We read in Ecclesiastes 2:18-23:

> I hated all my toil in which I had toiled under the sun, seeing that I must leave it to those who come after me—and who knows whether they will be wise or foolish? Yet they will be master of all for which I toiled and used my wisdom under the sun. This also is vanity. So I turned and gave my heart up to despair concerning all the toil of my labors under the sun, because sometimes one who has toiled with wisdom and knowledge and skill must leave all to be enjoyed by another who did not toil for it. This also is vanity and a great evil. What do mortals get from all the toil and strain with which they toil under the sun? For all their days are full of pain, and their work is a vexation; even at night their minds do not rest. This also is vanity.

There's more in Ecclesiastes 4:4-8, but it doesn't get any better.

> Then I saw that all toil and all skill in work come from one person's envy of another. This also is vanity and a chasing after wind. Fools fold their hands and consume their own flesh. Better is a handful with quiet than two handfuls with toil, and a chasing after wind. Again, I saw vanity under the sun: the case of solitary individuals, without sons or brothers; yet there is no end to all their toil, and their eyes are never satisfied with riches. "For whom am I toiling," they ask, "and depriving myself of pleasure?" This also is vanity and an unhappy business.

Not a pretty picture of work. So why do we clock in?

### We'll Die If We Don't!

Ecclesiastes says that fools fold their hands and die from laziness (4:5). So we work to stave off death brought on by lack of creature comforts. We work to put a roof over our heads and food on the table. Since the curse of Eden, we have been sweating in the dirt to secure our food from a hardscrabble ground that exacts a price on us in exchange for a crop. Maslow's hierarchy of need is true. We work to provide for basic human needs. An empty stomach can be a powerful motivator.

Which raises an interesting question: How do Christians understand a welfare system that houses and feeds those who can work but don't?

I don't think many Christians oppose a form of welfare that aids the orphan and the widow, the in-between-jobs provider, the incapacitated and injured, or the single parent with a load of child care. But what about the able-bodied-jobs-are-available lazy person? Does Ecclesiastes suggest that this person is a fool who should fold his or her hands and die? Are we required to remove the consequences for nonwork as an act of human compassion? Maybe our government has nullified the musings of Ecclesiastes by rewarding the refusal to work.

This is the kind of tension that work theologies bring on. Where do consequences for laziness end? And where does mercy begin? How does society require someone to work? How responsible is society for those who choose not to work? And who's to say that the single mother feeding her children on food stamps, helping them with homework, clipping coupons, and transporting her elderly mother to the doctor is not working as hard as any clock puncher? Work baptizes us into a river of theological questions.

If you had a roof over your head, food on the table, and basic medical care, would you still work? I suppose the question might be, "Who is the fool? The one who works and has these things, or the one who doesn't work and has these things?"

- In a barbaric world, the only option was work to survive.

- The ancient biblical community had a safety net in family customs as well as the command to love the neighbor and the stranger.
- The Puritan work ethic formed a society where shame kept people at work. Your ticket to belong in the community was punched only if you worked.
- Communism sought to level the playing field with all receiving the same from a power that created all labor.
- And the America of today is debating the size and responsibilities of the government for the people it taxes and governs.

I already hear the complaints rising from several quarters:
- "If minorities had the same access to good jobs as the white majority, things would be different." (Of course.)
- "Education affords some the things that others can never have." (Of course.)
- "Those who have are responsible for those who do not have." (The Bible seems to say something close to this.)
- "Does the Bible promote socialism or democracy?" (The case has been made both ways.)
- "Am I really my lazy brother's keeper?" (Depends.)

So on one level, Ecclesiastes may be right: we work because we'll die if we don't. This Maslow's hierarchy reason for work is probably the ground floor of our motivation for working. But working to eat to work to eat to work to eat seems like *hebel* to me. It is a fog that you live in but can never quite hold in your hand. You are here today, gone tomorrow. Is working for life's necessities all there is to our labor? Ecclesiastes suggests another reason.

## We Envy Each Other

Then I saw that all toil and all skill in work come from one person's envy of another. This also is vanity and a chasing after wind. (Ecclesiastes 4:4)

Work is how we compete. It is how we compare ourselves with others. Almost every field of labor has some measure of human performance by which we are ranked with our fellow humans—grade point average, win-loss record, sales, crop yield per acre, bank account, acquisitions, deals closed, volume.

I think it all started one day in a cave as two prehistoric brutes sat around a fire. One said, "Uga-buga one," and the other replied, "Uga-buga two," and the rat race was on.

The reality for many of us is that our work seems like vanishing fog, because ours compares poorly with others whose work is so much bigger, faster, and more glamorous. And some work very hard for no money at all, yet are assigned to devalued categories of unemployment. How does our work make us feel on the plane of human competition?

I remember when my youngest daughter was in grade school. During vocation week, the teacher invited the parents of students to come to the class and describe what they did for a living—without naming the job. Abby wanted me to come. Friday was my day to show up and describe my vocation.

As the week progressed, Abby became more anxious. I learned that I had been preceded by a fireman with a truck to climb on, a policeman with a gun and siren, and a zoologist with snakes. How could a preacher top that? I, also, was beginning to feel anxious. How do you make being a pastor cool to first graders?

I gave it my best—counseling people in trouble, visiting the sick to pray with them, speaking to congregations on Sunday. As I talked, the look on Abby's face seemed to say, "You're killing me, Dad!" At the end of my job description, the teacher asked, "So now, class, what is Mr. Boone's occupation?" The best guess on my occupation came from a bored child who said, "He goes places and says things."

The room was lifeless. Nobody guessed my vocation, and Abby had to bail me out. And then a kid asked if I did funerals. I reminded them in a movie-mocking voice, "I see dead people." After that, everything was cool. My work was interesting because I saw people dead. Take that, zoologist!

Have you noticed how some people can't wait to tell you what they do and others seem to apologize for it? Work puffs one chest full of pride and then lays a head on the same chest in shame. Some work esteems us while other work dis-teems us.

I know that Michael Jordan was devoted to his work as a basketball player. The competition drove him to a discipline rarely matched and caused him to play when he was sick as a dog. It mattered to him whether he won or lost; it mattered whether he was better than the other guy. "Love of the game" is how this is usually described.

But I wonder if love of self might be the more accurate description. Do we work to feel good about ourselves in comparison with other people? And is this part of the *gift* of work or the *curse* of work?

I lead a Christian university in Nashville, Tennessee. Trevecca Nazarene University has several sister faith-based colleges in Nashville. We are bigger than Welch College and the Sisters of Aquinas. We are smaller than Lipscomb and Belmont.

How do I know? I watch the numbers. And it steams me a little when we don't get the press coverage that our larger sisters get. I work a little harder to catch them or to be mentioned in the same story line. Am I envious? Does this envy motivate my work? Is this partnership with God, or is it the curse of working in a world where people are stacked on a totem pole of importance?

Maybe Ecclesiastes is right. We are envious. And we need some power greater than ourselves to redeem this motivation from becoming destructive—for ourselves and for others. And there's another reason we work.

## We Want to Be Remembered

I hated all my toil in which I had toiled under the sun, seeing that I must leave it to those who come after me—and who knows whether they will be wise or foolish? Yet they will be master of all for which I toiled and used my wisdom under the sun. This also is vanity. So I turned and gave my heart up to despair concerning all the toil of my labors under the sun, because sometimes one who has toiled with wisdom and knowledge and skill must leave all to be enjoyed by another who did not toil for it. This also is vanity and a great evil. What do mortals get from all the toil and strain with which they toil under the sun? For all their days are full of pain, and their work is a vexation; even at night their minds do not rest. This also is vanity. (Ecclesiastes 2:18-23)

We work to leave something behind. While anxious about who gets it and how it might be used, we still want to leave some evidence that we have mattered. Of all the things humans fear, one of the greatest is that we will be forgotten. We will live, strive, work, play, love, build, give, sweat, sing, care—and no one will remember. It scares us.

This fear is heard in the cries that have risen.

> Remember the Alamo.
> Remember Pearl Harbor.
> Remember 9-11.

We want to be remembered.

> It's why we built memorials at Normandy and Nagasaki.
> It's why people's names are engraved at the Vietnam Memorial and the Holocaust Museum.
> It's why pews and Bibles have names written on them and in them.
> It's why buildings are named and ex-presidents have libraries.
> It's why we have entities like the Barnum and Bailey Circus, the George Forman Grill, the Vince Lombardi Trophy, the Smithsonian Museum, and Rockefeller Center.

It's why college presidents can raise money for build-ings, programs, and scholarships by asking people how they would like to be remembered.

Deep in the human heart is the fear of being forgotten. Through our work, we are secretly hoping that we, too, will be remembered.

My plan for posterity was to leave behind hand-built fur-niture. I built bedroom sets for each of my three daughters: pencil post beds, drop-down desks, seven-drawer chests, and bed stools. I crafted these from the best pine I could afford and patterned them after the Shaker furniture that has stood the test of time. I even had my signature placed on a brand-ing tool and branded each piece: "Made by Dan Boone."

The plan was that my daughters would someday say to their children, "This furniture was made by my father. I used it when I was your age." And then they would say to their children, "This furniture was made by my grandfather, God rest his soul. I used it when I was your age." And they would say to my great-grandchildren, "This furniture was made by my great-grandfather, blessed be his memory to all, and I used it when I was your age. Look, his name is branded into the wood right here."

Allow me to share with you the path of that furniture. It went from their childhood bedrooms (until they became cool teenagers) to the family guest room (until we started having really important guests) to basement storage (until we ran out of space) to a yard sale (when we needed money for them to go to college).

I'm guessing that somewhere in the world this coming Saturday morning a person is making a seventh-hand-yard-sale purchase and wondering if this was really made by Daniel Boone.

I have questions.

• Is work the way we live forever?

- Can it really be done in such a way that they will still be talking about us when we are pushing up daisies?
- Does it matter to us what is said at our funerals regarding the kind of work we did? Is this why we work?
- And should we be anxious about what happens to the fruit of our labor after we are gone?
- Is it a godly thing to think now about a surviving widow's lifestyle, a grandchild's college education, a church's financial need, an institution's future?
- Is this love, or is it the human struggle to eat from the tree in the center of the garden and live forever?
- Will we die grudgingly, surrendering our wealth to the next generation, or expire in peace?

We ask a lot from our work—to feed and clothe us, to secure us, to make us feel comparable to our peers, to cause us to be remembered. And Ecclesiastes says it is all *hebel*—vapor, fog; here today, gone tomorrow.

I think I like the theology of work in country music better. At least we get to quit in style, like Johnny Paycheck.

But maybe there is more going on than we see in Ecclesiastes. It says one more thing about work in 5:18-20:

> This is what I have seen to be good: it is fitting to eat and drink and find enjoyment in all the toil with which one toils under the sun the few days of the life God gives us; for this is our lot. Likewise all to whom God gives wealth and possessions and whom he enables to enjoy them, and to accept their lot and find enjoyment in their toil—this is the gift of God. For they will scarcely brood over the days of their lives, because God keeps them occupied with the joy of their hearts.

At the core of Ecclesiastes' sarcasm and pessimism about work, there is wisdom. He seems to be saying that if we draw our life and identity from our work, if it tells us who and whose we are, if it is all we live for, we will end up holding fog someday. But if it is a gift from God that occupies us all our days with good things to do, and if we experience our work as given by God, and if we know we are blessed, then our life is rich.

|

— 2 —

# THE EVOLUTION
# OF WORK

|

A few years ago, David McKenna wrote a book in which he chronicled the evolution of American thought regarding work. In *Love Your Work* he notes five distinctive phases of thought and approach to our labor.[1]

1. Our forefathers and foremothers came to America with the **Puritan work ethic**. They believed that work was a calling from God. The word vocation stems from the Greek word *vocare*, "to call." When we hear ministers speak today of their divine calling, we are using the language that most Puritans used to speak of their vocations. Whatever their work, God had called them to it. The way they expressed worship to God was to fulfill their calling. Hard work was worship. Work sanctified a person and made that person holy. The very sacredness of a person before God was connected to the way he or she worked. Work was from God, for God, to God.

2. Benjamin Franklin's book, *Poor Richard's Almanac*, ushered in the second phase of American work. The

**craftsman ethic** was rooted in building the American society by making a contribution. Man depended on his skills, thrift, and ingenuity to make a contribution to the common good. "Early to bed, early to rise, makes a man healthy and wealthy and wise." We made our mark by being good craftsmen who took pride in our work. We contributed to a prosperous society by dedicating ourselves to our work. What society and others thought of us began to replace what God thought of our work. We worked for a better world.

3. In the 1800s, we entered a phase known as the **entrepreneurial ethic.** This was the age of the robber barons who seized control of capital and clawed their way to massive fortunes over the blood and bodies of craftsmen. They established a new goal for work—get rich, very rich. They worked in a world being created for their own advantage. Their brilliance was in recognizing where the world was headed and getting there first with transportation, product, or invention. While they brought many gifts to civilization, they did it more for themselves than for God's pleasure or society's good.

4. From the freelancing ways of the robber barons emerged the giant corporations of America and the **career ethic.** You went to school, earned a diploma, and became a company man or woman. As an organizational worker you climbed as far up the ladder as you could in the same company until your clock ran out or you retired with a gold watch. Conformity to the company ethos replaced craftsmanship. Profit sharing replaced entrepreneurial wealth. Cooperation replaced competition. And the separation of the sacred from the secular replaced doing your work for the glory of God.

5. And now we live in a world of the **self-development ethic**, where jobs are short-term transportation to get us to our dreams. We want the least amount of hassle

for the greatest reward. We are jealous of the person who has the "cushy" job, who has it "made in the shade." We hitch a ride to our destiny on the back of a job. Some have called them "McJobs," because we seem to drive by them quickly. We seek personal satisfaction, growth, good relationships, minimal interference, and benefits. We don't necessarily want to lead or follow. We just want interesting work that makes days pass fast. We want people to treat us kindly, to sympathize with our conflicting schedules, to understand us, and to be fair. The profit of the company ranks very low on our list of concerns, because we probably won't be around very long.

We've come a long way from the Puritan's divine calling to McJobs. Granted, the phases are not characteristic of everyone in each age. What makes some workers stand out is their commitment to one ethic in a different time—the Puritan working at McDonald's today would be a blessing to any manager.

We used to work for God; now we work for ourselves. We used to rest and recreate to energize us to do good work. Now we work to earn money to recreate and play.

Slowly, like a frog in a kettle, Christians have been shaped by our culture's prevailing theology of work, and we have permitted that ethic to become quasi-Christian. Tune in to religious broadcasting and you will hear a steady stream of "God wants you to have the desires of your heart. God wants to prosper you for the sake of driving the car you want, living in the house that 'is you,' having the body of a movie star. You are God's beloved and you deserve these things." And bits of this are true, when held in tension with other biblical realities.

But see how long you have to listen to hear anyone in religious broadcasting say that our work ethic is meant to reflect glory to God, or that Christians are called to some of the hardest tasks, because this is where the neighbor is served. I have listened long and hard for a sermon about work that builds a God-honoring society. The idea that our work is worship is never mentioned. In today's self-development, self-enrichment ethic, work is more like a necessary curse than a divine calling.

I think we have a better story than this.

Our story begins in a garden. Most people jump to chapter 3 of the Genesis garden story where the curse of sin results in child-bearing labor pains, weed-bearing soil, and sweat-of-the-brow work. A theology that quickly moves to the curse concludes that work is a necessary evil, a load put on us by a ticked-off God whose fruit tree got raided.

I remember pounding nails into asphalt shingles on a 100-degree Mississippi day with Uncle Lee. Between the grunts of his hammer blows, he huffed, "I just have one question for Adam and Eve. Was the apple really worth this?"

Our theology of work does not begin with Genesis 3 but with Genesis 1—2. The essence of our humanity is described in Genesis 2:7:

> Then the LORD God formed man [Adam or humankind] from the dust of the ground, and breathed into his nostrils the breath [Hebrew, *ruach*] of life; and the man became a living being [Hebrew, *nephesh*].

These Hebrew words are very important. *Nephesh* occurs 755 times in the Old Testament and is usually translated "soul." But there are other flavorings of the word that give us its fuller meaning. The root of the word is *throat* or *neck*. The *throat* is the primary organ for receiving air and water. It must remain open lest we die. The *throat* opens itself to life-sustaining substances—air, water, food. The word can also mean *neck*. This is the most vulnerable part of our body. It is a symbol of our fragility as humans. When we speak of being endangered, our *neck* is in the noose.

*Nephesh* is also translated as "desire, wanting something that lies outside you."

In many of the psalms, it is the word that defines a longing, a striving after, a wanting for, a thirsting quest. These meanings define us as needy, thirsty, vulnerable, and dependent. We are created as creatures with an inner need. We fill that need, temporarily, by way of an opening from inside our gut to the outside. In other words, we are not self-sustained creatures who can nourish and fulfill ourselves internally. We are aimed outward for that which we need to keep us alive.

Bob Wiley is needy. If his name sounds familiar to you, you've probably seen the movie *What About Bob?* Bob has every ailment known to humans, every phobia, every complex. He has driven his psychiatrist out of the profession and the exiting psychiatrist decides to refer Bob to his least-liked competitor, Dr. Leo Marvin. Dr. Marvin is the proud author of the recently released book *Baby Steps*. In his first session with Bob, Dr. Marvin successfully gets Bob to take a few baby steps of responsible action. Bob experiences the exhilaration of hope and decides that Dr. Marvin is the miracle worker he has been looking for all his life. The only problem: Dr. Marvin is about to go on a month-long vacation, and Bob will have to wait until he returns to proceed. Bob cannot wait. He tries everything to discover where Dr. Marvin is vacationing, and following multiple failed attempts, succeeds. He boards the bus to Lake Winnipesaukee, carrying his pet goldfish, Gill. As Bob arrives in the quaint lake village, Dr. Marvin is exiting the local grocery store with his family. They meet face-to-face. Dr. Marvin rebukes Bob sternly and tries to put him back on the bus. But Bob stands there declaring the pivotal words of the movie, "I need, I need, I need."

Bob has discovered something about himself. His *nephesh*. He is expressing the essence of his humanity, that he is a dependent being who cannot fulfill himself without aid from outside. When Bob Wiley says, "I need, I need, I need," he is being human.

According to Genesis 2, we are a walking thirst, an open throat, a vulnerable neck, a deep desire, a need. As dependent creatures, God has given us work that matches the essence of our humanity. In partnership with this God, we receive gifts via our throats—water, air, and food. We experience meaningful relationship in a sustaining partnership. We accept our fragility and dependence rather than seeking to overcome it. We are *nephesh*.

The other key Hebrew word in the Genesis text is *ruach*.

Then the LORD God formed man [Adam or humankind] from the dust of the ground, and breathed into his nostrils the breath [Hebrew, *ruach*] of life; and the man became a living being [Hebrew, *nephesh*].

We experience God internally as divine breath that jumpstarts these dust-formed bodies, these Claymation creations. Until God breathes life into us, we are dust. Life is gifted to us in the breath. It is no wonder that the third person of the Trinity is known as Holy *Ruach*/Spirit.

I have been in rooms where babies are born and in rooms where people die. One common reality is that the first breath is always in and the last breath is always out. We inhale at the beginning and exhale at the end. To be inspired is to be in-spirited. To expire is to be de-spirited. Our life is the rhythm of breathing—receiving life from God as gift to dependent creatures, returning life to God as worship/work. Inhale the gift, exhale the response of sacred work.

I have always suspected that the writer of *What About Bob?* was a theologian. Bob boards the bus with a fragile goldfish named Gill (breathing capacity), utterly dependent on Bob to feed him. Bob gets "being human" better than the esteemed, published Dr. Marvin. As the movie plays out, Dr. Marvin's ego caves in on him, landing him in a psych ward, while Bob goes on to be a blessing in the counseling field.

When we believe we can supersede our humanity, our neediness, we go nuts. When we receive life from God and return worship to God in the way we work, we find ourselves fully human.

We are created in love, placed in relationship with other humans, and given domain of a garden. We have responsibility for the animals, the trees, and the plants. We are partners with God and have staff meetings at the end of the day in the cool of the shade. We sharecrop. We have no needs that are not addressed by the Creator. We are zoologists, farmers, harvesters, chefs, horticulturists, and bird-watchers.

Our garden-variety sin was our desire to escape our humanity. Somehow the tree in the center of the garden is the focal point of our fall. It represented the opportunity to star in the role of God. We violated the boundary that God had set around the tree and listened to the serpent of self-centeredness. Before long we were hiding from God, covering up to protect ourselves from each other, blaming one another, and feeling distanced. The curse of Genesis 3 is not the action of God's anger, but rather the consequence of our choice. When we are not reconciled to God as dependent creatures, all human work gets complicated. The womb and the ground wrestle with us before yielding their fruit. We wrestle our life from them where we once opened our arms to receive the gifts of God.

Some have viewed work as the curse of the fall. The biblical picture of work (pre-fall Eden) is a delightful partnership. Work came before, not after, the fall. And even as we exited the garden, we did not cease to be capable of partnership with God. While our address is no longer Eden, we are still entrusted with the care of all creation. We are given skills for the work needed. We engineer, fix, build, write, teach, make music, paint, invest, manage, heal, serve, cook, transport, deliver, clean, entertain, solve, and counsel. This is good work.

Some have called it an occupation, because it occupies our time, thus distracting us from the reality that we have an expiration date. Ecclesiastes 5:18, 20 lends some credence to this.

> This is what I have seen to be good: it is fitting to eat and drink and find enjoyment in all the toil with which one toils under the sun the few days of the life God gives us; for this is our lot. . . . For they will scarcely brood over the days of their lives, because God keeps them occupied with the joy of their hearts.

Occupied, yes, but with the joy of our hearts. Our deepest joy is found in living as humans created by and for God, dependent on God, living in a working partnership with God. This exalted view of the human is much better than living for consumption and pleasure, or simply being occupied. I suppose this is the difference between an occupation and a calling—one diverts our attention from eternal reality, the other participates meaningfully in that reality.

Our calling is simple—to be saints. It is the invitation and purpose of God that we live lives of sacred intent by receiving life and returning worship/work. Our individual callings are varied. Some of us have music in us; some of us don't. Some of us think and reason mathematically. Some of us understand why people argue. Some of us are passionate about a more just society. Some of us like cars—selling them, fixing them, driving them. Some of us desire to serve public need through government organizations. Some of us are quick and accurate with computers, cash registers, and keyboards. Some of us want people to get well. Some of us love the look of a fresh-mowed lawn or a street cleared of trash. Some of us are energized by the classroom. Some of us wish to advocate for the single mother trying to make ends meet. Some of us love caring for our children.

These callings are doable within our bodies and gifts. We find joy in this work. We are more than occupied, we are invested. And this is one of the major venues, if not *the* major venue for expressing our gratitude to God for the gift of life.

|

— 3 —

# MOSES
## UNION ORGANIZER
## AND POLITICAL ACTIVIST

|

He told God he was not cut out for the job. Moses was scared spitless at making public speeches and even more scared of serving as the mouthpiece of God before the throne of Pharaoh. But his résumé clearly fit the role God had in mind for delivering the slaves from Egypt. Moses had been raised in Pharaoh's palace and knew the language, culture, and customs of the jobsite. He had been nursed and raised by a mother who was a slave—and thereby understood the predicament. A sense of justice had been instilled in him, causing him to defend an Israelite under attack. He had shown the courage to defend a minority against a member of the majority. And he knew, from his work with Jethro's flocks, how to lead a herd to water and food. So God called Moses to be a union organizer and political activist. He was a perfect fit for the job.

While it may seem that our work comes at us out of the blue, most of the time good work is done by people who are uniquely prepared to do it. We speak of this kind of work as our vocation, our divine calling. Many have written about vocation. Note the following:

Lester DeKoster: Work is the form in which we make ourselves useful to others.[1]

Ben Witherington III: Our vocation is how we participate in the coming kingdom and build the culture of that kingdom here and now.[2]

Miroslav Volf: Work is cooperation with God, in the Spirit, for the good of the neighbor.[3]

Dietrich Bonhoeffer: Vocation is the place at which one responds to the call of Christ and thus lives responsibly, taking a stance against the world within the world; it is responsibility that is wider than career, issues, relations, and places.[4]

Frederick Buechner: The kind of work God usually calls you to is the kind of work (a) that you most need to do and (b) that the world most needs to have done; the place God calls you to is the place where your deep gladness and the world's deep hunger meet.[5]

Dorothy Sayers: Vocation is a way of life in which one finds proper exercise and delight in the presence of God; it is creative activity undertaken for the love of the work itself and is a natural function of a person made in the image of God.[6]

N. T. Wright: Vocation is our participation in the new creation, building upon the foundation laid in Christ and thereby implementing the achievement of Jesus' resurrection; we are cross-bearers of the crucified love of Jesus working at the place where the world is in pain.[7]

I suppose Moses' experience fits all these, though he might disagree that delivering the slaves was the work he most needed to do. Like Jonah, he did his best to run the other way. Yet this work needed to be done. It involved the cross-bearing love of God, it participated in the future God was creating, it was a stance against the world from within the world, it was useful to others, and it was a delight to God.

I have friends who wish God would be this clear with them as to their calling. They have asked and prayed—but still no burning bush in the middle of their unemployment, no voice of God on the backside of the desert, no divine certainty of where to apply. When it comes to vocation, it seems that God speaks loudly to some, whispers to others, and is tight-lipped to the rest. I know lots of Christians who do good work and believe to this day they have never been called to clock in at their current worksite. Like Nike, they just do it.

But when it comes to vocation, is it dangerous to lean on our own understanding? How well do we know ourselves? How much do we know about the world we are going into? How much job experience does it take to know if you are good with numbers or a disaster at the cash register? Do vocational callings come after age thirty or before? Do we ever really know what we want to be when we grow up?

I was called to preach at age twelve. I heard a voice loud and clear. I said yes without contest. I was pastoring a church by age fifteen, preparing in college and seminary until age twenty-five, and in a full-time pulpit for twenty-eight years.

Then the phone call came to be considered for a college presidency. Was this my calling? It would certainly take me in a different direction. As I considered the possibility, it occurred to me that most of my pastoral life had been spent serving college congregations, that I loved the teaching opportunities I had had in these settings, that one of my strengths was communicating Christian faith to a questioning world, that I had served on numerous governance boards, that I had built buildings and raised money, and that I had led a large organization. A friend suggested that I had been perfectly prepared by God for this work.

I don't know. Other people under consideration could have done the job just as well or better. I could have been very happy to pastor until retirement. The college could have said, "Thanks for applying, but we are going a different direction." I could have been a professor of preaching and pastoral theology. But after eight years on the job (and writing this book during my first sabbatical ever), it seems to me that God has called me to what I am doing.

Maybe we understand vocation better looking in the rearview mirror. Has the work met our deep need or the world's deep hunger? Time will tell. Or maybe we have an overdeveloped sense of vocational anxiety. Maybe God confirms our calling as we put our hands to the tasks in front of us. Maybe we need to let our soul tell us whether there is joy and meaning in our work.

Barbara Brown Taylor writes:

One common problem for people who believe that God has one particular job in mind for them is that it is almost never the job they are presently doing. This means that those who are busiest trying to figure out God's purpose for their lives are often the least purposeful about the work they are already doing. They can look right through the people they work with, since those people are not players in the divine plan. They find ways to do their work without investing very much in it, since that work is not part of the divine plan. The mission to read God's mind becomes a strategy for keeping their minds off their present unhappiness, until they become like ghosts going through the motions of the people they once were but no longer wish to be.[8]

Barbara recommends getting beyond the ghostliness by engaging in manual labor. She suggests washing baseboards, dogs, or windows. These domestic arts have a tendency to return us to our senses.

I have experienced this escape into mowing the lawn. When my body is at its peak physical output, my mind has the opportunity to focus on the larger questions without overthinking. Sometimes the simplicity of the future that God desires is not that complicated. But we overcomplicate it with our needle-in-a-haystack anxiety that there is only one time clock in the world at which we are crafted to punch in. Really?

Maybe God has lots of work that we can do—in many places and with many people. I have developed my own folk theology of how God leads us toward careers. Please excuse my simplicity. It seems to me that God leads in one of three ways.

The first is **opened and closed doors**. I have rarely walked through a door that has not been opened to me, which seems to suggest that wanting a job that is not open to you is wasting time—at least for now.

God knows that as novice Christians, our discernment is frail. We are not ready to make life-altering decisions. So God makes it clear and simple. "Don't go there; go here." And we walk through the doors God opens, yielding ourselves to be God's servants in that place.

The second method of divine leadership is what I call **Ping-Pong balls in a bucket of water**. There are options, each like a single Ping-Pong ball. We submerge them in prayer and see which one keeps floating to the top. By holding them before God and asking God to help us see how we might be useful to him in each scenario, the preferred picture of our future emerges.

The third method is the **fruit of maturity**. We are committed to God, devoted to doing God's will and work. We have what Paul describes as "the mind of Christ." And with options on the table, God says to us, "I know your heart. Choose, and I will be with you." Sometimes God allows us to be the utility player who can cover second base or pinch-hit in the bottom of the ninth. And if the Psalmist is correct, God delights in giving us the desires of our heart. So why would God not be in something that excites every cell in our body?

I fear that we often view God as a power baron who wants to see if we will forsake what our heart, mind, soul, and strength longs to do just to prove that if God calls us to something despicably unfun, we would do it. I am not suggesting that there are never difficult jobs or that suffering will never be a key part of our calling. But I am questioning a view of God that leaves no room for us finding deep joy.

Having served a college-aged generation for the past twenty-eight years, I know the angst that accompanies the "what am I to do with my life?" question. I do not mean to demean the importance of the quest. But I do want to invite an anxious generation to calm down and believe that God is a good guide and can lead us on an excursion of many detours that may be as interesting and beneficial as heading straight to the perfect job the day after college graduation.

Again, from Barbara Brown Taylor:

When I cannot tell whether it is a sleeping cat or an engorged dust ball under my bed, I know that I have been spending too much time thinking. It is time to get down on my knees. After I have spent a whole morning ironing shirts, folding linens, rubbing orange-scented wax into wood, and cleaning dead bugs out of light fixtures, I can hear the whole house purring for the rest of the afternoon. I can often hear myself singing as well, satisfied with such simple, domestic purpose.

This is my practice, not yours, so please feel free to continue calling such work utter drudgery. The point is to find something that feeds your sense of purpose, and to be willing to look low for that purpose as well as high. It may be chopping wood and it may be running a corporation. Whatever it is, perhaps you will hold open the possibility that doing it is one way to learn what it means to become more fully human, as you press beyond being good to being good for something, in a world with the perfect job for someone like you.[9]

All this makes me wonder if Moses' life would have been easier if he had just replied to the smoldering bush, "Sure, sounds interesting. When do I start?"

|

— 4 —

# BEGINNING WITH THE END IN MIND

|

Stephen Covey has inspired us to live highly effective lives by incorporating specific habits. One of these habits is to begin with the end in mind.[1] He suggests that all things are created twice—once in our imagination, then in the world. A gymnast sees a completed routine in her mind and then replicates it. An artist forms a mental image and then transfers it to a canvas. A speaker watches a mental video of the talk he is about to give and walks onstage to talk it out.

This is not new. The Old Testament prophets operated this way centuries ago. As the mouthpieces of God, prophets lived near the heart of God. So near that the Spirit in them was aligned with the heart and mind of God. As intimate partners with God, they saw what God was doing in the world and understood the kind of future that God willed.

In other words, they began with the ending God had in mind and worked backward into the present. They were co-creators of the future with God through the words they spoke. Their addresses to the people commonly began, "Thus says the Lord . . ." What followed was a divinely preferred picture of the future—which we call prophecy.

Central to this way of thinking is a robust doctrine of creation. If one's theology of creation ends somewhere around Genesis 2 with a fully formed, predetermined outline of history, then it follows that we, as workers, are pawns in an already forecast story.

God-talk interests me. My friends often speak of God in mechanical, preplanned ways. They recount these opening chapters of Genesis like this:

> Before God made Adam and Eve, he already knew everything that was going to happen from that day to the end of time. He knew these two creatures were going to make a royal mess of things, but he went ahead and made them anyway. After they misbehaved, he kicked them out of the garden to let them know they couldn't get away with such behavior.

That's how I hear people tell this part of the story. Mechanical. No surprises. God arranged it all beforehand. God lined up the dominoes, tipped the first one into the second one, and let them fall in prearranged order. And I have trouble with that way of telling the story.

One Christmas, our family got hooked on a domino game called Mexican Train. You pile the dominoes in the middle of the table. Each player takes fifteen. The game begins by placing the double twelve in the middle of the table. Each player makes his or her own train off the double twelve. The strategy is to line up your dominoes in numeric order, connecting them in one straight line. You alone can play on your train. You hope to play each domino in order. But there are ways to mess people up. You can play a double on your train and leave it open. This means that the next person has to cover your open double before he can play anywhere else. Groans are heard as the player pulls a tile from the middle of perfectly arranged dominoes waiting to be played. Now there is a gap in the numerical sequence. Your train has been derailed by a rogue double. Your competitor has messed up your train.

As I read Genesis, God hadn't counted on the mess we made. It wasn't preplanned. God wasn't lining up historical dominoes for a solitaire game of domino tip-over. God was playing with partners. We played rogue dominoes on our train and God responded. This isn't how God intended the game to go. As I read our story, God created the world with a frightening freedom given to his creatures. But God also was possessed with a stubborn love that willed life for these creatures. God's loving insistence and stubborn persistence refused to throw in the towel on these creatures.

We are even treated to an insider view of the heart of God in the story of Noah. It suggests that had God known in Genesis 1 what God knew by Genesis 6, he would never have emptied the box of dominoes onto the table. God regrets that he made us (Genesis 6:6). God moves to blot out all of his creation with a cosmic eraser, the flood. But as the story unfolds, it is not in the heart of God to end his creation.

Rather, he moves to save it, even though his creatures have become sinful, violent, and deadly. From this moment on, God is on the move through the likes of covenants, prophets, priests, and kings to define the kind of future he is after.

As Christians, it is our calling to participate with God in the formation of the world God imagines, desires, and wills. In other words, we do our work with the end in mind. We envision God's desired future and then return to the present to enact it through our work.

This also requires a solid eschatology, a theology of last things. Our work is located in the middle of two theological bookends—creation and eschatology, beginning and ending. It is held in tension by the already and the not yet. We work in partnership with the God revealed in creation. We work with this God toward the day when the knowledge of God will cover the earth as the waters cover the sea.

Some have suggested that we are building the kingdom of God on earth. This may be too much to suggest. The idea that Christians will complete God's kingdom or that our obedience ushers in the kingdom as the crowning act of our work—well, history shows that this is not likely. For all the centuries of our clocked-in existence, we have not come close to eradicating evil. If anything, we have gotten better at filling the world with violence.

Rather than building the kingdom, we are receiving the kingdom into the present by our godly work. If the kingdom of God is coming toward us from the future, we can be opened to receive it here and now as an expression of the reality of God's in-breaking reign. This is how the ministry of Jesus is interpreted in the Gospels. As Jesus speaks and heals and casts out demons, the kingdom of God comes among them. This is why we pray, "Thy kingdom come. Thy will be done" (Matthew 6:10, KJV). It is the prayer that we might be the place where God's future is being lived out.

In the days of Isaiah, the nation was on the verge of collapse. The wealthy protected their interests at the cost of the poor. Judges were bribed at the city gates. Merchants used false scales to measure out goods. Land was confiscated, and the poor were ensnared in slavery. National security was pursued through conquest of weaker nations. And all of this was occurring under the guise of a covenant with God. These were "God-fearing people" who were attending temple worship and parading piety while living in violation of God's law. In Isaiah 1—6 we find a prophetic critique of their ways. But we also find something else—a vision of the future. Isaiah seeks to correct their actions by calling them to live with the end in mind, to see what God is working toward.

The word that Isaiah son of Amoz saw concerning Judah and Jerusalem: In the days to come the mountain of the Lord's house shall be established as the highest of the mountains, and shall be raised above the hills; all the nations shall stream to it. Many peoples shall come and say, "Come, let us go up to the mountain of the Lord, to the house of the God of Jacob; that he may teach us his ways and that we may walk in his paths." For out of Zion shall go forth instruction, and the word of the Lord from Jerusalem. He shall judge between the nations, and shall arbitrate for many peoples; they shall beat their swords into plowshares, and their spears into pruning hooks; nation shall not lift up sword against nation, neither shall they learn war any more. (Isaiah 2:1-4)

As these words fell on deaf ears and stone hearts, God removed the hedge of protection from the nation and allowed them to be taken as exiles into Babylon. They failed to repent of their evil practices. They refused to embrace a different future than the one they were creating. Had they listened, the way they worked would have changed dramatically.

Embedded in Isaiah's prophetic vision is a call to become a living model of the way of God. "The nations shall stream to it. Many peoples shall come and say, 'Come, let us go up to the mountain of the Lord, to the house of the God of Jacob; that he may teach us his ways and that we may walk in his paths'" (2:2-3).

What would it look like for Christians to do their daily work as if they were teaching the whole world how to work? Nations would stream to the people of God to learn their ways. Our work would be exemplary. We would perform our daily tasks in a way that would serve as instruction for others.

I am thinking of the man who works at the water purification plant. His attention to gauges and chemicals and processes is the kind of work that protects the water supply of a community. He may do his work alone, out of public view, but what if he sensed the call of God to work with the kind of attentive diligence that, if replicated by others around the world, would save thousands from disease and death? What if his work were an example for others, an inspiration to his fellow employees, a picture of how the community water treatment facility would be operated in the kingdom to come? What if his work empowered him to volunteer to a small city in a third world area and help them establish a water treatment facility and train its employees?

As a college president, I often ask business owners to make internships available for our students. I am convinced that learning occurs through hands-on experience. We learn through the pores of our body as well as the cells of our brain. When a worker is asked to accept an intern, that worker often experiences esteem in their work. They are given the opportunity to share their wealth of knowledge with another human. Someone comes to them to learn how to do something. To teach another person how to work is an affirmation of our humanity.

In Isaiah, the people of God were cheating each other at the weight scales, hoping no one saw. They bribed a judge, hoping no one was listening. But if they could have seen themselves as teaching models of commerce and justice in the world, maybe their work would have been worthy of replication.

The kind of world God is building informs how we do our work. The failure of many sermons is that they do not identify the workplace as a site of imagined obedience. The kingdom of God can come in a water treatment facility just as it can come in a Bible study, and maybe more.

Isaiah's vision also suggests that peace among peoples is the goal of our work. "He shall judge between the nations, and shall arbitrate for many peoples; they shall beat their swords into plowshares, and their spears into pruning hooks; nation shall not lift up sword against nation, neither shall they learn war any more" (2:4).

Rather than contributing to the division in the world, our work would arbitrate differences in partnership with God. Rather than making weapons of destruction, or bombs to drop on people, or gossip to harm the guy down the hall, we would be looking to turn destructive energy into peaceful work.

Take hatred, divisiveness, and conflict out of the workplace and imagine the productivity. It requires massive energy to keep a feud going. I have often wondered what the world would look like today if all the money spent on wars in Afghanistan and Iraq had been spent on education, job training, and health initiatives in third world countries. I am not suggesting that evil does not at times require a military response, but I am suggesting that the work of the kingdom is peacemaking to the core.

The people of God clock in as peacemakers in the world. The bank teller interacts with an angry employee. Does she speak words of peace into his or her day? Does she champion processes that make it easier for customers? Does she arbitrate differences between employees and create the kind of work atmosphere in which conflict is resolved? What might it look like for swords to become plowshares, company weapons to become creative tools?

A factory was closed in Michigan and employees were offered positions in a sister company factory in Tennessee. The resident southerners were suspicious of the northern newcomers, believing the company intended to pit the two groups against each other and eliminate the slackers. Animosity arose in the plant, creating tension and turf wars.

Productivity plummeted, and when asked, each side blamed the other. A Christian in the factory became concerned and went to management asking what was going on. Given assurance that the company desired to double the goods produced and that there was no plot to eliminate jobs, the believer sought divine wisdom for the division.

The God of creativity led the employee to begin Thursday night cookouts at his house, inviting two northern families and two southern families, kids and all, to join them for supper. Every Thursday night, four families sat around a backyard picnic table and told their stories to each other as their kids played in the yard. No work speeches about unity or getting along were made by the host—just gracious hospitality and good conversation. Slowly but surely, the workplace changed. Friendships formed. Suspicion disappeared. Productivity skyrocketed.

This is the vision of God for the working world. Sometimes we fail to believe that God speaks into the practices of the workplace. In the sanctuary on Sunday morning about our ethics, yes; but in the factory on Tuesday afternoon about a problem in shipping, we don't know. Yet here is God in the days of Isaiah, speaking to his people about commerce, business practices, and violence.

Later in Isaiah, as the exiles are returning from Babylon to rebuild their ruined cities, the prophet imagines again the future of God. It is an economic vision of a thriving community.

> For I am about to create new heavens and a new earth; the former things shall not be remembered or come to mind. But be glad and rejoice forever in what I am creating; for I am about to create Jerusalem as a joy, and its people as a delight. I will rejoice in Jerusalem, and delight in my people; no more shall the sound of weeping be heard in it, or the cry of distress. No more shall there be in it an infant that lives but a few days, or an old person who does not live out a lifetime; for one who dies at a hundred years shall be considered a youth, and one who falls short of a hundred shall be considered accursed. They shall build houses and inhabit them; they shall plant vineyards and eat their fruit. They shall not build and another inhabit; they shall not plant and another eat; for like the days of a tree shall the days of my

people be, and my chosen shall long enjoy the work of their hands. They shall not labor in vain or bear children for calamity; for they shall be offspring blessed by the LORD—and their descendants as well. Before they call I will answer, while they are yet speaking I will hear. The wolf and the lamb shall feed together, the lion shall eat straw like the ox; but the serpent—its food shall be dust! They shall not hurt or destroy on all my holy mountain, says the LORD. (Isaiah 65:17-25)

Does it occur to you that of all the occupations necessary for God's vision to be fulfilled, nothing is said about church-based occupations in this text? We are hearing about human thriving that requires good doctors, nurses, midwives, pediatricians, geriatric specialists, dieticians, baby-sitters, exercise therapists, masseurs, nursing home care-givers, in-home nurses, medical transcriptionists, pharmacists, chemists, radiologists, counselors, gardeners, farmers, food processors, grocery store managers, cooks . . . the list is long. All these skills and more are needed for babies to survive infancy and humans to live to a ripe old age.

This is God's desired future for us, and it delights God when we begin with the end in mind. God rejoices over us.

Imagine the kind of work we would do if we really viewed God as our employer and ourselves as God's partners in creation. At the end of each task done with excellence, God would smile—and we would see it. For a job well done, God would say, "You pleased me by the attention you gave to that." At the climax of an invention that would aid food production in drought-stricken nations, God would extend his hand for a high five.

I know this kind of language attributes human features to a far-beyond-human God, but this God finds deep joy in our work, and we should experience this joy. If the telephone company can deliver an understandable message, certainly

God can. The question is, are we experiencing the joy of God over our work?

Good work participates in the future that God is forming. Hope is nothing more than obedience stretching itself into the future, expecting to find the activity of God.

|

— 5 —

# THE "GODS" THAT
# HAVE TO BE CARRIED

|

I am a Star Trek fan. One of the most interesting charac-ters is a ruthless intergalactic conqueror called The Borg. These part human, part machine creatures all possess the same brain. They are part of a collective consciousness, all thinking the same thing at the same time. Their coordinated killing power makes them unstoppable. Their threat to the next planet is always the same line: "Resistance is futile; you will be assimilated." And from the body parts of conquered people, they made more Borg.

The Babylonians were the Borg of Old Testament days, taking the best and brightest of conquered people and as-similating them into Babylonian culture. The message was simple: Resistance is futile; you will be assimilated. It was a brain drain on the defeated culture and a shot in the arm for the conquering culture. And the assumption was that the gods of the victors had given them the victory. Babylon was god-rich with divinities like Bel-Marduk, Nebo, and Tiamat. The exiles, the best and brightest people of God, were con-stantly reminded of the "superior gods" of Babylon.

In our post-Christian America exile, we are surrounded by gods who intend to assimilate us into their way of thinking. They claim to be our creators, kings, and rulers of culture. They are hoisted on shoulders and regularly paraded before us. And we are being slowly seduced to believe—

- The gods of advertising who tell us that our happiness is packaged in a product
- The gods of materialism who tell us we are what we earn and own
- The gods of fashion who dictate our clothing budget
- The gods of success who teach us to manipulate each other
- The gods of consumption who strip the earth bare and leave nothing for our children
- The gods of debt who tell us we should have it now
- The gods of alcohol and drugs who numb us
- The gods of sexual expression who champion one-night stands over covenanted marriage bonds
- The gods of politics who make promises that can't be kept
- The gods of power who tell us we should never suffer
- The gods of prestige who crown television idols and icons
- The gods of sports who rule our schedules more than a Christian calendar
- The gods of fame who invite us to be the next Survivor, American Idol, or dancing star

They are everywhere! What do we do with them? Isaiah has a suggestion. Examine the gods that are handmade and see if they really are life-givers or just life-takers. He writes:

All those who make no-god idols don't amount to a thing, and what they work so hard at making is nothing. Their little puppet-gods see nothing and know nothing— they're total embarrassments! Who would bother making gods that can't do anything, that can't *"god"*? Watch all the no-god worshipers hide their faces in shame. Watch the no-god makers slink off humiliated when their idols fail them. Get them out here in the open. Make them face God-reality. The blacksmith makes his no-god, works it over in his forge, hammering it on his anvil—such hard work! He works away, fatigued with hunger and thirst. The woodworker draws up plans for his no-god, traces it on a block of wood. He shapes it with chisels and planes into human shape—a beautiful woman, a handsome man, ready to be placed in a chapel. He first cuts down a cedar, or maybe picks out a pine or oak, and lets it grow strong in the forest, nourished by the rain. Then it can serve a double purpose: Part he uses as firewood for keeping warm and baking bread; from the other part he makes a god that he worships—carves it into a god shape and prays before it. With half he makes a fire to warm himself and barbecue his supper. He eats his fill and sits back satisfied with his stomach full and his feet warmed by the fire: "Ah, this is life." And he still has half left for a god, made to his personal design—a handy, convenient no-god to worship whenever so inclined. Whenever the need strikes him he prays to it, "Save me. You're my god." Pretty stupid, wouldn't you say? Don't they have eyes in their heads? Are their brains working at all? Doesn't it occur to them to say, "Half of this tree I used for firewood: I baked bread, roasted meat, and enjoyed a good meal. And now I've used the rest to make an abominable no-god. Here I am praying to a stick of wood!" This lover of emptiness, of nothing, is so out of touch with reality, so far gone, that he can't even look at what he's doing, can't even look at the no-god stick of wood in his hand and say, "This is crazy." (Isaiah 44:9-20, TM)

When the work of our hands becomes the object of our worship, we have become idol-makers and idol-worshippers. This culture believes in our capacity to make that which can save us. The Borg is on the move assimilating us into cultures that bow to handmade gods.

How shall we respond? Isaiah suggests that we laugh. Here comes Cyrus the Persian, God's tool of deliverance, into Babylon to set the exiles free. The Babylonians realize their demise is imminent and they go running to their temple. The cry goes up among them, "Save the gods! Save the gods!" Can you see the Babylonians hauling out their handmade gods, Bel-Marduk and Nebo, lugging these "things" from their protected perches and strapping them onto the backs of mules and donkeys? Can you see these animals bowing low (sarcasm for worship) under the weight of these gods? Can you see them hustling these beasts of burden into the hills to spare their gods from being captured by Cyrus and becoming a trophy in his collection?

> Bel bows down, Nebo stoops, their idols are on beasts and cattle; these things you carry are loaded as burdens on weary animals. They stoop, they bow down together; they cannot save the burden, but themselves go into captivity. (Isaiah 46:1-2)

Do you see what the prophet is doing? He is poking fun at their gods, making a joke of them, laughing at them. This is sarcasm at its best.

Isaiah is teaching us to laugh at gods of our exiled culture. Why? Because gods who are created by humans have to be saved by humans. But the God who created humans does not have to be saved by humans. The gods who have to be carried cannot carry. The gods who have to be borne by beasts of burden cannot bear us as their burden.

Our God, the one who is doing a new thing, the one who is our Maker and Creator, says,

> Listen to me, O house of Jacob, all the remnant of the house of Israel, who have been borne by me from your birth, carried from the womb; even to your old age I am he, even when you turn gray I will carry you. I have

made, and I will bear; I will carry and will save. (Isaiah 46:3-4)

The gods of our hands have no life in them. We made them. We must carry them, sell them, stock them, ship them, fuss over them, repair them, protect them, defend them, and worship them. Our God is different. Our God carries us. His ways may surprise and startle us. His ways may be new. But his ways are saving.

People who have to carry and protect and defend and save their gods are anxious, worried, fearful, weighed down.

Does this describe much of the American workplace today? A site where mere mortals believe they are actually creating that which can save them and carry them? When work product is elevated to the level of a god, we have entrusted our lives to something that we must continually give life to.

But work that worships the living God places us in the arms of one who can carry us. This work is hopeful, looking for every sign of God at work doing a new thing.

|

— 6 —

# THE SIZE OF OUR WORK

|

*Afghanistan, listen to me. Russia, France,*
*Zimbabwe, pay attention to what I'm saying.*
*Singapore, open your ears. Australia, this is*
*something you really need to hear.*

You would think me strange to call the nations of the
earth to pay attention to what I am about to say in this
chapter. Truth is, they aren't paying attention to me. They
have no clue I'm even here.

This is how Isaiah 49 begins. The Servant of the Lord
says, "Listen to me, O coastlands, pay attention, you peoples
from far away!" (Isaiah 49:1a).

Who is this Servant-of-the-Lord stranger who believes
his work is so important that all the nations ought to sit up
and take notice? We get his bio in the following verses.

The LORD called me before I was born, while I was in
my mother's womb he named me. He made my mouth
like a sharp sword, in the shadow of his hand he hid me;
he made me a polished arrow, in his quiver he hid me
away. And he said to me, "You are my servant, Israel, in
whom I will be glorified." (Isaiah 49:1b-3)

This Servant of the Lord reminds us of other characters we have known. Jeremiah, the one called while still in the womb. Sarah's baby, born to parents far past childbearing years. The prophets of Israel, given sharp tongues.

Who is this Servant? A person or a people? Is the Servant past, present, or future? Does the Servant speak for God or to God or as God? Clearly, from the bio, we know that the Servant is called and sent by God, belongs to God, and has the stated mission to glorify God. And we New Testament folk who read this today think it sounds a lot like Jesus.

It probably doesn't matter to us whether we decide that the Servant of the Lord is a prophet, a people, or the coming Messiah—because this speaks to all of us. We are the servants of the Lord. We belong to God. We've been called. We are expected to bring glory to God. The work of the God-servant is world changing. The whole world should be listening.

But when we get to Isaiah 49:4, the Servant is in deep despair. Nothing is working out. Everything he touches breaks. His words are dull, not sharp. His arrow-messages don't hit the target. So he says: "I have labored in vain, I have spent my strength for nothing and vanity."

Sounds like a resignation speech in the making, because sometimes, well—there's not much to show for our work. Are you ready to quit? Resign?

I expect that Isaiah's servant was feeling something like that when he confessed his own failure to God. Expecting to be fired, or at least retired, and replaced by someone more equal to the task, he tells God that he has accomplished nothing, is nothing, deserves nothing; but God does not accept his resignation. God, whose ideas of success and failure have never coincided with our own, has a better idea. "I will give you as a light to the nations," God says, "that my salvation may reach to the end of the earth" (Isaiah 49:6).

Now that is divine logic for you. Fail at a large task and you are given a larger one. Produce hardly a spark in your own corner of the world, and you are promoted to light up the whole planet. It is either a case of divine irony or else God knows something we servants do not know—namely, that our success does not depend on those who are chosen but on the One who chooses them, the Holy One of Israel, in whose hand the sharp sword cannot fail to dazzle, in whose bow the polished arrow cannot fail to find its mark.

The only way we can truly fail, apparently, is to remove ourselves from those hands, to let our own poor judgment make us quit our relationship with the Chooser, disqualifying ourselves from God's service on the grounds that our efforts are not good enough, our skills are not fine enough, our scores are not high enough."[1]
Israel had narrowed her focus to the cause of getting back home to Jerusalem, restoring the fortunes of Jacob. She could only imagine a narrow Jewish agenda.

And now the LORD says, who formed me in the womb to be his servant, to bring Jacob back to him . . . he says, "It is too light a thing that you should be my servant to raise up the tribes of Jacob and to restore the survivors of Israel; I will give you as a light to the nations, that my salvation may reach to the end of the earth." (Isaiah 49:5-6)
God tells his servant, who feels like a total failure, that he has set his sights on too small a work, too light a challenge, too little a task. This happens so easily in exile. We shrink, hope shrinks, our mission shrinks.

For our work to be meaningful, we must understand how it connects to what God is doing in the world. This does not mean that our work is narrowly spiritual or evangelistic or churchy.

The minimum-wage nursing home assistant washes the body of an Alzheimer's patient who can neither appreciate nor express gratitude for the act. Yet, this worker is the compassion of God at work on behalf of a fragile human.

The cable television phone salesperson explains the benefits of the package her company offers to a person who does not know the difference between DSL, HD, LED, or DVR. This person is the truth-speaking help of God being offered to another human.

The waiter at Ruby Tuesday's takes an order, serves the table with care, and brings a meal to a traveling couple. He is the presence of God in kindness to a family en route to their father's funeral.

All work worthy of being done is in some way the activity of God. The seeming insignificance of it only reveals a lack of Christian imagination. Good work participates with the God who is always clocked in as a worker. Our small work is not beneath God, because God is no stranger to small. God does small quite well. You remember our stories.

- A childless old couple named Abram and Sarah
- Forgotten slaves in Pharaoh's mud pits
- A tiny band of survivors in the wilderness
- Gideon's subtracted army
- Little Samuel sleeping near the ark of Lord
- David, the runt of the litter, who took down Goliath
- A pregnant teenager named Mary
- Twelve followers you would never have picked
- A boy with five loaves and two fish
- The widow's mite
- A crucified Messiah bound in graveclothes, sealed in a tomb
- Disciples huddled in fear, knees knocking
- Seven scrawny churches in Revelation facing the Roman Empire

God doesn't need us to be big. He just needs us to realize that *our work is big.*

God will not adjust his work to our interests. God invites us to adjust our interests to his work. God is redeeming the whole world through the workplace.

Do we want in on it?

Maybe our work is not too insignificant. Our God is just too small.

|

— 7 —

# CHANNELING PROVERBS

|

I am a fan of three writers on leadership, all tempered by one faithful, pastoral theologian. The three writers are Jim Collins, Stephen Covey, and Warren Bennis. When I read their books, I feel wiser. I've passed their books around to the people I work with and insisted that we read and talk about the concepts. The pastoral theologian that I throw into the batch is Eugene Peterson. His reflections are those of the cynic who suggests that corporate thinking may be the death of the church. Mix all four together and you have some good stuff.

Why is it that I feel wiser when I read these leadership gurus? I suspect they may be channeling Proverbs, that ancient collection of wisdom.

Ray Dunning, my primary theological mentor, taught me that there are two strands of theological narratives in Scripture—redemption theology and creation theology.

- Redemption theology is mainly about getting slaves to freedom and sinners to deliverance. It is the story of turning Abraham into a people, getting the Israelites out of Egypt/Babylon, and the kingdom of God arriving full-bodied in Jesus to seek and save the lost.

• Creation theology is about the movement of the world from chaos to order. It suggests that there is a divine code embedded in creation such that things work best when they function as they were intended to. We find this story in the Wisdom literature, primarily Proverbs.

In his introduction to Proverbs in *The Message*, Eugene Peterson writes,

Many people think that what's written in the Bible has mostly to do with getting people into heaven—getting right with God, saving their eternal souls. It does have to do with that, of course, but mostly not. It is equally concerned with living on this earth—living well, living in robust sanity.

Wisdom is the biblical term for on-this-earth-as-it-is-in-heaven everyday living. Wisdom is the art of living skillfully in whatever actual conditions we find ourselves. It has virtually nothing to do with information as such, with knowledge as such. A college degree is no certification of wisdom—nor is it primarily concerned with keeping us out of moral mud puddles, although it does have a profound moral effect upon us.

Wisdom has to do with becoming skillful in honoring our parents and raising our children, handling our money and conducting our sexual lives, going to work and exercising leadership, using words well and treating friends kindly, eating and drinking healthily, cultivating emotions within ourselves and attitudes toward others that make for peace. Threaded through all these items is the insistence that the way we think of and respond to God is the most practical thing we do. In matters of everyday practicality, nothing, absolutely nothing, takes precedence over God.[1]

To be "Proverbial" is to be rooted in the fear of the Lord. This doesn't mean we hide under the bed when we hear God coming, but that we take God seriously as the source of life.

Creation theology tells a story of cause and effect, action and consequence. If we participate in chaos, we experience the paycheck of chaos. If we align ourselves with order, we experience the blessing of life as it was meant to be. In Proverbs, there are two roles that can be played—the wise one and the fool. To be the fool is to go against the grain of the world as God created it and intended it.

We learn wisdom by profound respect for God and God's ways. Wisdom is revealed to us through natural observation. Watch the slacker work and see what happens to him. Watch the cheat down at the muffler shop rip people off and see how much business he has a year from now. Watch the diligent worker perform tasks with timely excellence and follow his or her promoted trail. If we observe people, we will learn what is wise and what is foolish, because consequences follow actions.

In Proverbs, Wisdom is personified as a beautiful woman who is pursuing us, even as folly is personified as a prostitute who lures us down her dark streets. In other words, life is not neutral. There are forces at work to lead us toward life or death. We must choose the path we will walk. If we trust in the Lord with all our heart and are not intoxicated by our own opinion or sovereignty, the Lord will direct our path.

Wisdom personified beckons us in Proverbs 8:22-36, TM:

> GOD sovereignly made me—the first, the basic—before he did anything else. I was brought into being a long time ago, well before Earth got its start. I arrived on the scene before Ocean, yes, even before Springs and Rivers and Lakes. Before Mountains were sculpted and Hills took shape, I was already there, newborn; long before GOD stretched out Earth's Horizons, and tended to the minute details of Soil and Weather, and set Sky firmly in place, I was there. When he mapped and gave borders to wild Ocean, built the vast vault of Heaven, and installed the fountains that fed Ocean, when he drew a

boundary for Sea, posted a sign that said NO TRESPASS-ING, and then staked out Earth's Foundations, I was right there with him, making sure everything fit. Day after day I was there, with my joyful applause, always enjoying his company, delighted with the world of things and creatures, happily celebrating the human family. So, my dear friends, listen carefully; those who embrace these my ways are most blessed. Mark a life of discipline and live wisely; don't squander your precious life. Blessed the man, blessed the woman, who listens to me, awake and ready for me each morning, alert and responsive as I start my day's work. When you find me, you find life, real life, to say nothing of GOD's good pleasure. But if you wrong me, you damage your very soul; when you reject me, you're flirting with death.

With such a résumé, who are mere mortals to refuse the counsel of Wisdom?

Proverbs also displays deep respect for the traditions of the elders—the observant old ones who have much to teach us. The wise ones sit at their feet with ears open and mouths closed. And those whose lives have been blessed by God are a gift to their offspring—if the young bucks will listen.

Wisdom for work is ours to be had if we respect God, observe the consequences of human actions, pursue Wisdom as she pursues us, and listen to observant elders. When the wise go to work in Proverbs, diligence is present. The world ordered by such workers will be righteous and just. But when the fool goes to work, we hear words like *sluggard*, *lazy*, and *useless*. The world formed by them is all wrong.

Derek Kidner offers this summary of the sluggard:

The sluggard in Proverbs is a figure of tragic-comedy, with his sheer animal laziness (he is more than anchored to his bed: he is *hinged* to it, 26:14), his preposterous excuses ("there is a lion outside!" 26:13; 22:13) and his final helplessness.

**1. He will not begin things.** When we ask him (6:9, 10) "How long . . . ? When . . . ?" we are being too definite for him. He doesn't know. All he knows is his delicious drowsiness; all he asks is a little respite. . . . He does not commit himself to a refusal, but deceives himself by the smallness of his surrenders. So, by inches and minutes, his opportunity slips away.

**2. He will not finish things.** The rare effort of beginning has been too much; the impulse dies. So his quarry goes bad on him (12:27) and his meal goes cold on him (19:24; 26:15).

**3. He will not face things.** He comes to believe his own excuses (perhaps there is a lion out there), and to rationalize his laziness; for he is wiser in his own conceit than seven men who can render a reason (26:16). Because he makes a habit of the soft choice (he "will not plow by reason of the cold," 20:4) his character suffers as much as his business, so that he is implied in 15:19 to be fundamentally dishonest.

**4. Consequently he is restless.** (13:4; 21:25, 26) with unsatisfied desire; *helpless* in face of the tangle of his affairs, which are like a "hedge of thorns" (15:19); and *useless*—expensively (18:9) and exasperatingly (10:26)—to any who must employ him. . . .

The wise man will learn while there is time. He knows that the sluggard is no freak, but, as often as not, an ordinary man who has made too many excuses, too many refusals and too many postponements. It has all been imperceptible, and as pleasant, as falling asleep.[2]

A sampling of Proverbs describing the lazy worker confirms Kidner's comments.

You lazy fool, look at an ant. Watch it closely; let it teach you a thing or two. Nobody has to tell it what to do. All summer it stores up food; at harvest it stockpiles provisions. So how long are you going to laze around doing nothing? How long before you get out of bed? A nap here, a nap there, a day off here, a day off there, sit back, take it easy—do you know what comes next? Just this: You can look forward to a dirt-poor life, poverty your permanent houseguest! (Proverbs 6:6-11, TM)

Sloth makes you poor; diligence brings wealth. (Proverbs 10:4, TM)

Make hay while the sun shines—that's smart; go fishing during harvest—that's stupid. (Proverbs 10:5, TM)

A lazy employee will give you nothing but trouble; it's vinegar in the mouth, smoke in the eyes. (Proverbs 10:26, TM)

God hates cheating in the marketplace; he loves it when business is aboveboard. (Proverbs 11:1, TM)

Bad work gets paid with a bad check; good work gets solid pay. (Proverbs 11:18, TM)

Loafers say, "It's dangerous out there! Tigers are prowling the streets!" and then pull the covers back over their heads. Just as a door turns on its hinges, so a lazybones turns back over in bed. A shiftless sluggard puts his fork in the pie, but is too lazy to lift it to his mouth. Dreamers fantasize their self-importance; they think they are smarter than a whole college faculty. (Proverbs 26:13-16, TM)

A farmer too lazy to plant in the spring has nothing to harvest in the fall. (Proverbs 20:4, TM)

Don't be too fond of sleep; you'll end up in the poorhouse. Wake up and get up; then there'll be food on the table. (Proverbs 20:13, TM)

Slack habits and sloppy work are as bad as vandalism. (Proverbs 18:9, TM)

Life collapses on loafers; lazybones go hungry. (Proverbs 19:15, TM)

One of my favorite uncles was a man of uncommon wisdom and humor. His education was not a college degree but a life of rich experiences. Uncle Lee died too early. He was a man of proverbial wisdom.

His furniture company had an employee named Leroy who could have been the poster child for the sluggard of Proverbs. One day Leroy quit. When asked about who would fill Leroy's vacancy, Uncle Lee replied, "Leroy didn't leave a vacancy."

Humorous, but true. And quite sad. When our work occupies no space, meets no need, and leaves no mark, have we really worked?

|

— 8 —

# SLOTH

This chapter is adapted from *Seven Deadly Sins: The Uncomfortable Truth* by Dan Boone (Beacon Hill Press of Kansas City, 2008). Used by permission.

|

I f it isn't a two-toed creature, what is it? Sloth is . . .

Hitting the snooze button repeatedly
Drinking straight from the milk jug
Leaving dirty clothes on the floor
A love affair with the remote control
Never returning calls or writing thank-you notes
Leaving exactly two sheets on the toilet paper roll
Falling asleep every night to late-night TV
Living for sports
Tenured professors coasting intellectually
Troubled marriages passing on the marriage retreat
Knowing TV characters better than family members
Preaching other people's sermons
Wandering the mall, killing time, mastering small talk
Amusing ourselves to death
Letting discipline slide

Indifference
Wanting to live somewhere else all the time
Staying busy to avoid serious thought
Preoccupation with misery
Boredom in daily routines
Not caring, acedia
Inability to sustain interest in anything challenging
Feeling overwhelmed, and therefore, doing nothing
Sloppy, undisciplined thinking
Resignation from responsibility for others
Letting others make my choices
Going with the flow
Surrendering hope
Lethargy
Apathy
Spiritual amnesia
A deadly sin.

That's sloth. And it started in a garden. Every deadly sin has its origin in Eden.

The story goes like this. With the repetitiveness of a ticking clock, humans live their lives in cycles.

Morning. Evening.
Morning. Evening.
Sleep. Work.
Sleep. Work.
Empty. Full
Empty. Full.

The connection between creature and Creator is rhythmic. And the chief end of man is to worship God and enjoy him forever while working in the garden as a caretaker of creation. But Adam and Eve want more. If they can transcend their humanity, they will not be bound to the cycle of human living. They can escape the routine. The snake tells them it is possible. Eat from the tree in the center of the garden and they can make their own arrangements. They can reinvent the wheel, which hasn't even been invented yet. Life can follow their whims and wishes. They can be independent creatures, filling their lives with excitement on demand.

So they ate.

And they were still empty inside. But they needed a paycheck to buy the filler that would eliminate their emptiness. So they worked for enough money to stuff themselves—food, television, Xbox, the latest Grisham novel, South Beach Diet, stock market, power shopping, sexual conquest, idol worship, *Survivor*—anything to fill the void. We've always believed we could consume enough to make the emptiness go away permanently.

Slowly, something begins to happen to us as we keep filling the God-shaped hole with stuff. We grow tired, cynical, weary, and numb. All these momentary diversions and thrills no longer excite. An emptiness settles in, and it won't go away. Despair follows. We no longer care. We no longer feel responsible. We no longer want to try.

Some deadly sins can be done in a flash. We have to work up to sloth. Like cement, it takes a while to harden.

Some say sloth finds us midlife. Until then we're too busy chasing forbidden fruit. Such fruit must be tasted and digested several times before we despair of it. That's why it is thought of as a midlife sin. But then, I work on a university campus, and I've seen some young versions of the old sin. Just writing about it makes me tired.

And God's response to sloth? Daily routine. Adam and Eve are sent into a world of farming and child-rearing. Those who have done these can vouch for their repetitiveness. Till the soil, plant the seed, weed the plants, harvest the crop, put the crop away, get ready for next year. Have a baby, stay up at night with the baby, feed the baby, change the baby, put the baby down for a nap, change the baby, feed the baby.

Add to this the laundry, which mates in the closet while you aren't looking. It never ends!

We want magic fruit, miracle formula, instant fix, a change-your-life-forever seminar. And God gives us daily routines. We came from dust, we farm dust, we eat food from dust, which returns to dust by way of the public sewer system, until we follow the food we eat back into the grave. Dust to dust. Ashes to ashes. So goes our life under the sun.

No wonder the writer/philosopher of Ecclesiastes called it *hebel*—the Hebrew word for smoke, nothingness, vapor, hot air. Meaningless, that's what life is.

Smoke, nothing but smoke.
There's nothing to anything—it's all smoke.
What's there to show for a lifetime of work,
a lifetime of working your fingers to the bone?
One generation goes its way, the next one arrives,
but nothing changes—it's business as usual for
old planet earth.
The sun comes up and the sun goes down,
then does it again, and again—the same old round.
The wind blows south, the wind blows north.
Around and around and around it blows,
blowing this way, then that—the whirling, erratic wind.
All the rivers flow into the sea,
but the sea never fills up.
The rivers keep flowing to the same old place,
and then start all over and do it again.
Everything's boring, utterly boring—
no one can find any meaning in it.
Boring to the eye,
boring to the ear.
What was will be again,
what happened will happen again.
There's nothing new on this earth.
Year after year it's the same old thing.

Does someone call out, "Hey, *this* is new"?
Don't get excited—it's the same old story.
Nobody remembers what happened yesterday.
And the things that will happen tomorrow?
Nobody'll remember them either.
Don't count on being remembered.
(Ecclesiastes 1:2-11, TM)

It's easy to see why Adam and Eve didn't like the arrangement. Routine can be monotonous. Get up. Brush your teeth. Deal with your whiskers one way or the other. Bathe a body that won't stay clean. Feed yourself through one inlet and empty yourself through others. Gas up a car that will soon be empty again. Wash clothes that will need to be washed again. Drive the same road that you will return on. Fill out a report, again. Do the lesson plan that you will do for another class this time next year. Shine a light in an ear. Open the hood. Call a prospect. Market the product. Tend the store. Keep the assembly line running. Write the sermon. Routine. Life is made up of routine. Sloth is easily within our reach.

Bored with life, we begin to shirk our responsibilities and care less. We hate life in this armpit town. We resent the demands people make of us. We want to be left alone in our deserved apathy.

For weeks at a time we go through the motions, never seriously attending to God, never focusing on God, never turning ourselves over to God. The thought that by such negligence we keep on wounding the only being who loves us with a perfect and expensive love—these thoughts become bearable and then routine.[1]

Enlarge our life? Get out some? Been there. Done that. Too tired to try. Go away, please, just go away. You are bothering me. What do I want? Excitement. Ecstasy. Fantasy. Fulfillment. A high. A buzz. Elevation beyond the daily routine. But nothing works. It's all smoke.

God's response to this? More daily routine. Because God will not erase our *earthiness*. We are made with the capacity to be repeatedly filled and emptied. We are replenished daily, with enticing eternity in full view. And God has chosen to meet with us, and to give us life, and to be present with us, and to complete us . . . in the daily routines.

The routines that bore us are the workplaces where God has promised to meet with us. The routines we want to escape are the places where God becomes flesh and dwells among us. We want instant excitement; God gives us our daily bread. "The steadfast love of the LORD never ceases, his mercies never come to an end; they are new every morning" (Lamentations 3:22-23). Hope in the Lord, child, now and forever. Our path to an eternally exciting tomorrow is through the routines of today.

Ours is a God of pots and pans, lesson plans, common work, daily bread, care for the neighbor, care for the body. The things we wish to transcend are God's sacred meeting places. Sloth would just as soon skip the encounter. Sloth has already decided that no good thing can come out of responsible routines.

God is the beginning and end of our journey out of sloth. It begins when a light of hope penetrates the stupor of sloth's gloom. "I woke; the dungeon flamed with light! / My chains fell off; my heart was free. / I rose, went forth, and followed Thee." Maybe that's how it happens. The grace that precedes our freedom penetrates the darkness of despair. The move to liberate us begins outside us. Sloth exhausts the capacity to try. We need saving, and we will not save ourselves. Because we simply can't.

God, however, can. Because God is holy love, unstoppable passion. God desires for his creatures life that is—well, life.

God wants not slaves but intelligent children. God wants from us not numb obedience but devoted freedom, creativity, and energy. . . .

In short, we are to become responsible beings: people to whom God can entrust deep and worthy assignments, expecting us to make something significant of them— expecting us to make something significant of our lives. . . . We have been called to undertake the stewardship of a good creation, to create sturdy and buoyant families that pulse with the give and take of the generations. We are expected to show hospitality to strangers and to express gratitude to friends and teachers. We have been assigned to seek justice for our neighbors and, wherever we can, to relieve them from the tyranny of their suffering. . . .

For such undertakings we have to find emotional and spiritual funding from the very God who assigns them, turning our faces towards God's light so that we may be drawn to it, warmed by it, bathed in it, revitalized by it.[2]

This vibrant life of partnership with God is described in Romans 12:9-18. What seems a punch list for Christians is actually the opposite of sloth—a responsible discipleship, a Christlike life.

Love from the center of who you are; don't fake it. Run for dear life from evil; hold on for dear life to good. Be good friends who love deeply; practice playing second fiddle. Don't burn out; keep yourselves fueled and aflame. Be alert servants of the Master, cheerfully expectant. Don't quit in hard times; pray all the harder. Help needy Christians; be inventive in hospitality. Bless your enemies; no cursing under your breath. Laugh with your happy friends when they're happy; share tears when they're down. Get along with each other; don't be stuck-up. Make friends with nobodies; don't be the great somebody. Don't hit back; discover beauty in everyone. If you've got it in you, get along with everybody. (TM)

God's gift of routine work is the cure for sloth.

|

— 9 —

# WORDS IN THE WORKPLACE

|

Workplaces are made up of people, and these people converse at numerous crossroads. Simply put, conversation crossroads are places where people talk and tell what they know. Bug a conversational crossroad, and you can detect the quality of life in that workplace. God cares about what we say in the workplace.

From the writing of Paul to the Ephesians:

Let no evil talk come out of your mouths, but only what is useful for building up, as there is need, so that your words may give grace to those who hear. And do not grieve the Holy Spirit of God, with which you were marked with a seal for the day of redemption. Put away from you all bitterness and wrath and anger and wrangling and slander, together with all malice, and be kind to one another, tenderhearted, forgiving one another, as God in Christ has forgiven you. Therefore be imitators of God, as beloved children, and live in love, as Christ loved us and gave himself up for us, a fragrant offering and sacrifice to God. (4:29—5:2)

Condense that extremely long sentence and you get:
- No evil talk out of your mouth
- No words that tear down
- No words empty of grace
- No gossip; no slander; no malice.

Let's take a trip to two conversational crossroads found in today's workplaces. The first is **Piranha Pond**, and the second is **Gossip Graveyard**.

### Piranha Pond

On the surface, Piranha Pond looks like your average recreational lake. You can swim in it, fish in it, and boat on it, but unbeknownst to the casual observer, this pond is deadly. It is teeming with deadly, ferocious fish, called piranhas. Piranhas are beautiful from the side, a silvery blue color. They are oval from tip to tip, and flat and thin from gill to gill. Their average length is about the length of the human tongue.

From the side, piranhas might resemble a big, blue guppy; but from the front, you get a very different impression. Chances are, though, that you'll never come face-to-face with one. You'll never see them directly in front of you until it's too late. And only then will you discover that they have very strong jaws and their teeth are like spikes, the bottom ones fitting between the top ones like shearing scissors. This gives them a strong grip and tearing power. Head-on they aren't pretty to look at. They are simply effective and deadly.

I know a college professor who keeps a piranha in his office. He tells me that when you isolate piranhas, they lose their aggressiveness. You see, piranhas usually travel in schools—piranha packs. And they team up to prey on the weak. When they see a floundering fish, they swarm. Any hint of weakness, any sign of vulnerability, any signal of struggle, and it's a feeding frenzy.

Surviving in the workplace is tough enough for weak and injured people, but working in a Piranha Pond is deadly. You may want to steer clear of Piranha Pond if you've recently been demoted or divorced. You'll want to stay out of the water if you don't measure up to the company wonder child or if your self-esteem is fragile. And failure? The piranhas can smell it a mile away, so don't even stand on the shore if you've failed at a recent project. Instead, steel your emotions, seal your pain, smile through your tears, and suck it up. If you want to survive life in or near Piranha Pond, act as though you are in charge. No limping, no floundering, no vulnerability, and no failure, or you could be dead meat. It's sad what happens to people who live and work in Piranha Pond—they learn not to be genuine.

But maybe you're thinking, *That's not me; I'm not weak; I'm not a failure.* Well, let me share another fact with you. Piranhas have also been known to attack the strong. And when they attack the strong, the bigger the better. It doesn't matter how much success, money, prestige, position, or power you have; meat is meat. It's the way of life down at Piranha Pond.

They've been known to reduce a healthy person to bones in a matter of minutes. There are lots of skeletons at the bottom of Piranha Pond. The few who escaped the attack and lived to tell about it can show you their scars. Chunks of them are missing.

There ought to be signs posted around the pond, warning signs like "Piranhas live here." "Swim at your own risk." But unfortunately, there aren't any signs.

The scariest thing is that Piranha Ponds are everywhere. They're as small as two people with cell phones, a casual conversation over coffee, a front seat, the copy room, or a break room. And some of them are as large as the Internet. With our current technology, piranhas are plugged in, hooked up, and networked. They send e-mail, they're on Facebook, they are on Twitter, they blog, they are LinkedIn, they make calls, they send letters, they schmooze and work crowds, they leave anonymous notes, they text—all because it makes their work easier and more deadly.

If you dare, go down to the pond someday and drop an underwater microphone in the middle of their conversations. You'll discover some fascinating things.

- Piranhas have instant recall of entire conversations.
- They remember and can reproduce perfect voice inflections.
- They can discern the motives behind words and the plots behind deeds.
- They will tell you not only what was said but also what was meant by it.
- They are clairvoyant.

I will let you in on a little secret, though. For all their ferociousness, they're actually very insecure. Confront them and they'll back down. Get them alone and they lose their aggressiveness. They are actually sad little creatures with very strong jaws and voracious appetites that they don't know how to fill. They find security only in packs of those who think like they think.

The Piranha Pond—where often is heard a disparaging word, and the waters stay bloody all day.

## Gossip Graveyard

Come with me to a second place, another conversational crossroad. It's called Gossip Graveyard. It's very quiet. Not even a whisper can be heard. It's surrounded by a fence, and no phone lines run in or out. Worn out news is buried there. Gossip is laid to rest. Words without constructive value lie six feet under. Take a stroll around Gossip Graveyard and read the tombstones. Each tells a story.

**Here lies a rumor stopped dead in its tracks by the truth**. I love the story behind this one. A new employee wanted the job of a longtime employee and began to spread rumors about her relationship with the boss. Insinuations were made. But friends who knew the seasoned employee confronted the liar. The rumor was laid to rest.

*Here lies the attack on the character of a godly man.* This one is strange. A Christian was in a bar consoling a new friend whose dad had died. Someone who didn't like him insinuated that he was an alcoholic, but his boss got to the bottom of the rumor and cleared his name.

*Here lies the last conversation with a former friend of loose-tongued persuasion.* Wonder what happened there?

*Here lies a dark secret, a past sin, confessed, forgiven and forgotten.* Someone heard a confession and kept confidence.

*Here lies idle phone chatter.* Two people decided to change their topic of conversation for the better.

*Here lies a razor-sharp wit that had specialized in sarcasm.* That one is easy enough to figure out.

The tombstones go on. *Here lies a buried hatchet. Here lies the chip on a shoulder. Here lies slander.* I love strolling through Gossip Graveyard and reading the inscriptions. How did this stuff get here?

The faithful patrons of Gossip Graveyard quietly brought them here, buried them, and walked away. They could have taken this stuff down to Piranha Pond, thrown it in, made a big splash, and fueled the feeding frenzy. But they did the decent thing, the right thing, and gave it a decent burial.

The patrons of Gossip Graveyard get very little notoriety for their deeds. Most people will never know they knew. Most people don't even see the defining moment when they start to speak and are checked by a still, small voice, and gossip dies on the spot. But God notices and smiles.

The patrons of Gossip Graveyard get their kicks from seeing people walk around whole. They love seeing leaders who are respected, vulnerable people cared for gently, touchy situations handled face-to-face, and squabbles quickly settled. The patrons of Gossip Graveyard are also environmentally conscious—they dispose of trash when they see it. They safeguard the health of the workplace. They believe that every person is an image-bearer of God and by grace capable of love.

Although these patrons may be quiet, they are brave. They've been known to wrestle a juicy piece of meat from the jaws of the piranha. At times, they've even confronted piranhas face-to-face. They have the marks to show for it. The patrons of Gossip Graveyard are trustworthy.

- They are keepers of character.
- They are truth-tellers.
- Their hearts are predisposed to trust.
- Their words build people up.
- Their offices invite honesty.
- Their friends are real.
- They foster places where people want to work.

And just as every community has a Piranha Pond, every community has a Gossip Graveyard. And the two places couldn't be more different.

The words we say reveal our hearts.

When God says, "Open your mouth and say *aaaahhhh*," he sees past our tongues, past our vocal cords. He sees our hearts. Our words are the windows of our souls. So God offers us the option of a healthy workplace. God is the forgiver of our sin, the guiding nudge before our next word, the sanctifier of our word-producing heart, and the custodian of community who hears each word we speak. God gets involved in our speech.

The moment of choice, a defining moment, comes to all of us. We stand daily at conversational crossroads with two potential paths—Piranha Pond or Gossip Graveyard. Where will we take what we know? What will we do with those meaty things called words? What kind of workplace will we build?

|

— 10 —

# WHEN WORK IS A PAIN

|

I f you want to promise people that hard work is rewarded, Proverbs is the goldmine of texts. But it is not the only voice that speaks into the workplace. The Old Testament story of Job is a dissenting voice to the wisdom of Proverbs. Job lived proverbially, did everything he was supposed to do, and lost it all.

Some have suggested that Job was written as protest to the proverbial promise that if we do "a" we will get "b." Sometimes we do what is right and suffer for it. Job's friends all had PhDs in wisdom but were declared by God to be dead wrong. Suffice it to say there is no divine guarantee that if we do the right things we will get the results we want. There is rogue suffering in our world, and sometimes our vocation finds us right in the middle of it.

Moses' life would have been more serene tending sheep on Horeb, but God called him to work in a place where babies were being smothered, humans were treated like dirt, and power vested against freedom. Moses was given no leverage except the word of the Lord. The case can be made that, similar to Job, it all turned out well in the end. But Moses never got to wiggle his toes in Promised Land dirt or dance the jig of freedom. He did the heavy lifting, and others tasted the joy.

Paul, formerly known as Saul, is another case in point. His résumé as a worker for God would include:

- Five floggings of thirty-nine lashes each
- Three times beaten with rods
- One stoning
- Three shipwrecked nights
- One day and night adrift in the open sea
- Significant experience in dangerous situations (bandits, wilderness, enemies)
- Work settings characterized by sleep deprivation, starvation, nakedness
- Experience in escaping death threats
- Rival leaders in the organization
- False characterization (big talk, little action)
- Numerous imprisonments
- Trial experience in Roman courts
- Death sentence.

I'm not sure any of us have a résumé like this. But we do have our own experiences in the workplace. At times, we work in places marked by sexual harassment, bullying, demeaning put-downs, favoritism, violence, cruelty, unreasonable demands, ungodly work hours, back-stabbing comments, energy-draining days, and spirit-debilitating bosses. In short, we suffer.

Those who plan church services would do well to pay more attention to the lament psalms of the Bible. Too often, services are designed to pump us up and get us all standing on our happy feet, clapping and singing at the top of our lungs, which is not bad. But many people walk into a church building wishing that other Christians would acknowledge the difficult place they have spent the last five or six days. They need some outlet for confessing that their work is often dehumanizing, robbing them of any identity, measuring them by output alone. They have been anonymous cogs in a machine, enslaved for far too many hours in a care-less environment. They have been cussed out, beaten down, and crushed. They do not ask that the whole church throw a pity party for them, but they do wish the church would give voice to the suffering that occurs in the workplaces of the people of God.

As a pastor, I always tried to give honest voice to the bad news in the world.[1] We did this several ways: drama that depicted the things people do to each other, news clips of human suffering, testimonials, man-on-the-street interviews about things that hurt people, movie clips demonstrating the reality of sin in the world.

In a series on the seven deadly sins, we came to the topic of greed. It would have been easy to decry greed from the pulpit, but I chose to show a movie clip from *Wall Street*. Gordon Gekko, the unscrupulous corporate raider played by Michael Douglas, was making a riveting speech claiming that greed is good. It was the essence of the world's opinion on greed, spoken out loud, in the sanctuary. While a few congregants protested giving service time to such an unchristian message, others expressed their appreciation that we were willing to recognize the reality they had to work under.

I proceeded to challenge the assumptions of the movie through a sermon on the parable of the man who built bigger barns. One congregant told me at the close of the service that he worked for a Gekko-like boss. He had lived under the brute force of this man—until today. God met him in his suffering with grace for the workplace.

We bring our workplace road dust into the sanctuary of God, hoping that God cares. In addition to things done to us, we also bring our own issues from navigating the workplace:

grasping anxiety
mouthy words about others

attitudes toward authority
marital frustrations and fissures
sexual temptations
prejudice
tendency to nitpick people raw
festering wounds
misuse of power
bodily abuse
selfish posturing
lies of overestimation and flattery
secret dark places
preoccupation with image
love of money

These things don't stick out in the world's shadowy work-lands, but put them under the blazing searchlight of God, and they stick out like a Volkswagen on a Mercedes lot. And if our *personal* hearts are clean and clear of sin-driven suffering, then our *corporate* hearts still need to confess on behalf of others. None of us has graduated from praying the Lord's Prayer. "Forgive *us* [corporately and personally] *our* trespasses, as *we* forgive those who trespass against *us*."

When we name and confess these sinful behaviors, a watching world will know how we feel about suffering in the workplace. We live as servants of Jesus in a sinful culture. The road dust of this world clings to our feet. We are not untouched by the evil around us. If we view ourselves as Christian escape artists who slither through the Monday to Saturday work world, unfazed by its seduction and influence, we are only fooling ourselves. We must name the influences, behaviors, and powers that run a dark world. We must confess before God that we suffer, that we sin, and that we need cleansing.

There is a brokenness among us that must be brought before God. We have been hurt, lied to, taken advantage of, manipulated, raped, stabbed in the back, neglected, divorced, robbed. What shall we do with this stuff? The world offers no place to take it. The church invites people to bring it with them to corporate worship and confess it to God.

It is healthy to admit what is wrong in front of God. We can say right out loud that our lives aren't what we'd hoped they'd be. Or even more, what God wants them to be. We can admit that our workplaces are stained by darkness. We can declare that we hurt deep inside. We can utter our sickness and grief, our failure and sin. We can admit what is bad about the world we live in. Rogue suffering is real.

Paul knew it when he was being beaten. We know it when we are being cussed out. While it would be easy to protest that our suffering is not the same as Paul's (because he suffered for preaching the gospel of Jesus), we need to realize that our suffering comes from the same dark powers as his. We suffer in the workplace because the kingdoms of this world have not yet become the kingdom of God. We suffer because evil still lurks in the hearts of people. We suffer because darkness is threatened by light. And the way we respond to our suffering is just as much a witness to the new world coming as Paul's sermons were in his day.

Too often our prayers are for a better job. Working at a Christian university, I receive countless résumés and appeals from people who have been beaten up in the world and are willing to work for less money in a Christian environment. I remind them that suffering is still possible when you work among Christians. I have seen as much pain in Christian institutions as in non-Christian workplaces. Sometimes the wounds are deeper when they come under the guise of faith. Maybe our prayers are not for deliverance from these hard places but for courage to be God's person in the middle of them.

I am not suggesting that suffering entails quiet complicity with wrongful treatment. Being quiet in the face of human destruction is rarely the way of God.

I keep a copy of Martin Luther King's *Letter from Birmingham Jail* on my desk. His model of nonviolent resistance to evil is profoundly Christlike. He was arrested as an outside agitator for coming over from Atlanta to meddle in the racial affairs of Birmingham. In writing from jail to his captors about the interrelatedness of all people, he penned these words, "I cannot sit idly by in Atlanta and not be concerned about what happens in Birmingham. Injustice anywhere is a threat to justice everywhere. We are caught in an inescapable network of mutuality tied in a single garment of destiny. Whatever affects one directly affects all indirectly."[2]

Our suffering is to be in keeping with the suffering of Jesus, which culminates in crucifixion and resurrection. This is our calling, our vocation in the world. We bear the pain of the world so that the crucified love of Christ may be experienced through us.

The Christian vocation is to be in prayer, in the Spirit, at the place where the world is in pain; and as we embrace that vocation, we discover it to be the way of following Christ, shaped according to his messianic vocation to the cross, with arms outstretched, holding simultaneously to the pain of the world and to the love of God.[3]

What if our deepest fellowship with God is sharing in the suffering of Christ where we work, in hope of resurrection to a new way in the workplace? What if we prayed for wisdom to respond to evil boldly, for strength from the Spirit to endure, and for tact to act rightly for the sake of all involved?

Well, we might get fired. Or we may experience the kingdom of God nosing its way into the present from the future. I am not suggesting that we are the messiah for everything broken or that Monday morning we give the boss a piece of our mind about his lousy ethics. I am suggesting that our walk with God affords us wisdom from the Scriptures, friends in the faith, and guidance from prayers to know how and when to respond to evil in the workplace.

Some work is hard because evil people are present. But some work is hard because the work is difficult. Imagine sitting at the bedside of a dying spouse as life passes you by. No one knows you are there, and the one you are tending has Alzheimer's and cannot appreciate the sacrifice of your laid-down life. Or the person who tends the interstate tollbooth in the sweltering summer heat. People hate paying the toll and view you as the despised toll collector. And you are anonymous to all who pass by, caring less about your day than their dollar. Or the shoe salesman who once ran a small business but now shoves too-small shoes onto the stinky feet of women who are sure they can still get into a size 6. Or being an undocumented person who works in constant fear of deportation. Some work is just hard.

But God is known to go to hard places, small places, insignificant places. The question about Jesus, "Can anything good come out of Nazareth?" was a way of asking a profound question about an insignificant place. If God is at work in Nazareth, maybe he is at work at the bedside of an Alzheimer's patient or in a tollbooth or in a shoe store.

|

— 11 —

# BLESSING

|

I must admit to some prejudice on this topic. I twitch when I hear a megachurch television preacher talk about blessing. Sometimes I move from twitching to retching. When a sermon makes a single desirous individual the lone person at the bottom of God's big blessing funnel, ready to receive all the wealth, health, and wisdom that God has, in exchange for a seed of faith (money) planted in the coffer of a preacher under investigation by the IRS for fraudulent reporting of income, which supports his overly lavish, consumptively ridiculous lifestyle—well, I want to throw up. And it makes me even sicker to see the faces of those who pack the auditorium for their weekly worship experience. Okay. There. I have that out of my system.

Blessing is a primary biblical theme. It begins in the creation story as God blesses living creatures, sea monsters, winged birds, and two clay-made humans. God declares them good and blesses them. God also blesses the seventh day as a day of rest to all his creation. God's blessing falls on animals, people, and time.

In Scripture, a blessing is *words invested with the power to do good*. Its dark cousin, the curse, is *words invested with the power to harm*. In the Old Testament, words are deeds. They go out from the one who speaks them and cause something to happen, good or bad. The word of the Lord created the world. The curse of Balaam put a whammy on the military might of tribes. Words do things. And when God speaks blessing, God is affirming the life that is being sustained by divine breath. Blessing is the validation of the existence of something. It is like a bow wrapped around a box, making it a gift highly treasured.

Words of blessing drip with life. Words of cursing smell of death's decay. Moses addressed the people of God in this way:

> See, I am setting before you today a blessing and a curse: the blessing, if you obey the commandments of the Lord your God that I am commanding you today; and the curse, if you do not obey the commandments of the Lord your God, but turn from the way that I am commanding you today, to follow other gods that you have not known. (Deuteronomy 11:26-28)

God's words can give life, and they can bring on the death we have chosen to partner with. Christians have chosen to live under God's blessing.

Abram was the recipient of a blessing that formed a people who are still in existence to this day, as national culture (the Jews) and as a Christian people (the church). Both point to the things said to Abram as their heritage.

> Go from your country and your kindred and your father's house to the land that I will show you. I will make of you a great nation, and I will bless you, and make your name great, so that you will be a blessing. I will bless those who bless you, and the one who curses you I will curse; and in you all the families of the earth shall be blessed. (Genesis 12:1-3)

God's intent was to bless the entire world, all the families of the earth, through Abram. Blessing has its eye on the neighbor, the stranger, the competitor, the boss, the janitor, the immigrant, the customer, the stockholder, the lender, the homeless. Blessing was never meant to be dammed up in a reservoir of self-keeping. It is God's way of extending his life to all.

If you follow the story line of Scripture, it is apparent that the worst times for the people of God were the times they hoarded the blessing of God for themselves. They cheated each other in the marketplace with crooked scales and balances. They bribed the judges. They confiscated the land of the poor. They loaned money to the poor with exorbitant interest. The rich became richer and the poor poorer as a result of their single-minded accumulation of wealth. And the prophets denounced them.

By the time of Jesus, the world was made up of those who were "blessed by God" (money, wealth, power, prestige, religious acceptance into the temple pecking order, pure lineage, male) and those who felt "cursed by God" (tax collectors, prostitutes, the lepers, sick folk, handicapped folk, sheep herders, women) because they were barred from blessing. And along came Jesus announcing a new sheriff in town. He brought a new reign called the kingdom of God. Characteristic of this new kingdom was a reversal of fortunes. Outsiders were in for good news. This was their lucky day, because the kingdom of God had come for the likes of the cursed. In the Beatitudes, blessing falls on the poor in spirit, the mourners, the meek, those hungering for a fair world, the merciful, the peacemakers, the persecuted.

He looked up at his disciples and said: Blessed are you who are poor, for yours is the kingdom of God. Blessed are you who are hungry now, for you will be filled. Blessed are you who weep now, for you will laugh. Blessed are you when people hate you, and when they exclude you, revile you, and defame you on account of the Son of Man. Rejoice in that day and leap for joy, for surely your reward is great in heaven; for that is what their ancestors did to the prophets. But cursed are you who are rich, for you have received your consolation. Woe to you who are full now, for you will be hungry. Woe to you who are laughing now, for you will mourn and weep. Woe to you when all speak well of you, for that is what their ancestors did to the false prophets. (Luke 6:20-26)

In the new deal called the kingdom of God, blessing is offered to those who never considered themselves eligible. Cursed are those who believe their blessings are their own doing for their own pleasure. This new arrangement is not about a socialist state where the playing field is leveled by the government and everyone gets the same paycheck. Nor is it about the evils of being wealthy, fed, and happy. It is about access to the blessing of God.

The religious system of Jesus' day had denied access to certain classes and groups of people, and they were living under the belief that God hated them. Jesus brought good news to everyone. Well, maybe not everyone. Those who still desired to build religious fences to protect their own interests at the expense of the neighbor would find themselves misaligned with the new kingdom.

A language pattern of blessing emerges in several of the Gospel stories. The same formula is found at the feeding of the multitudes and the Last Supper. Each time, Jesus *took the bread, blessed it, broke it, and gave it to his disciples.* The pattern of the bread mirrored the pattern of Jesus' life. What was done to bread was also done to Jesus.

The Father *took* Jesus into his love, laid claim to him in the womb of Mary as the holy child. Jesus was aware of his chosenness, his takenness, from early days. His Father had work for him to do. Even as a child in Jerusalem sitting with the elders in the temple, he knew himself to be about his Father's business.

The Father *blessed* Jesus. At his baptism the heavens opened, a dove came down and landed on him, and words of divine favor were spoken. "This is my Son, the Beloved, with whom I am well pleased" (Matthew 3:17). The Father pronounced Jesus as treasured gift, beloved Son, the blessed one. Under the power of this blessing, Jesus was able to move into the world offering blessing to all. Never did "being blessed" become something that was all about him. He stood in the stream of the Father's abundant love and offered the living water to all who came to him thirsty.

And Jesus was also *broken* by the Father. What was done to bread was done to Jesus. He was not shielded nor sheltered from the cruelty of a cursing world. He felt the pain of rejection, denial, betrayal, injustice, torture, and crucifixion. In the words of the religious sentiment of his day, "Cursed is the one who dies on a cross." Jesus went to the cursed cross and died there in our place. In other words, what broke Jesus into pieces was his willingness to do the work of the Father in places where life was being taken from people. Suffering in the workplace is the way of God in the world. Brokenness is not something "in the way" of success. It "is the way" of a successful Christian life. To avoid being broken by a cursing world is to take a path other than the one footmarked by Jesus.

In the resurrection, the Father who has *taken* Jesus, *blessed* Jesus, and *broken* Jesus, now *gives Jesus away*. His resurrected life is God's gift of blessing to all who believe in him. I find it interesting that Jesus does not pause for a victory lap at the mouth of the tomb. This is the site of Pilate's sealed warning to all that the powers in charge are not to be messed with. Had I been the scriptwriter, I would have had Jesus standing on top of the rolled-away stone, delivering a message about who is really in charge of the world. Instead, we find an angel left behind with a message for his disciples. If you want to follow him, he is already on the road to Galilee (where the work of God in a cursing world needs to be done). We can go find him there if we are ready to get to work.

Amy Sherman, in her book *Kingdom Calling: Vocational Stewardship for the Common Good*, suggests:

> Jesus' work is not exclusively about our individual salvation, but about the cosmic redemption and renewal of all things. It is not just about our reconciliation to a holy God—though that is the beautiful center of it. It is also about our reconciliation with one another and with creation itself. . . . This too-narrow gospel focuses believers missionally only on the work of soul winning. It has little to say about Jesus' holistic ministry or the comprehensive nature of his work of restoration. It focuses on the problem of personal sin only, thus intimating that sanctification is a matter only of personal morality (rather than that plus social justice). It focuses believers on getting a ticket to heaven, but doesn't say much about what their life in this world should look like. Put differently, it focuses only on what we've been saved *from*, rather than also telling us what we're saved *for*.[1]

If we rightly comprehend blessing, our vocation is much more than a career. It is the call of God to live under the awareness that we are chosen and treasured, beloved and blessed, broken and bruised, all for the purpose of being given away as the blessing of God for others. Our vocation entails how we spend money, who we have sex with, how we do our work, what kind of citizens we are, how we tend our lawn, and what our neighbor thinks of living beside somebody like us. Vocation is most often associated with our job because we spend more time there than any other single endeavor. But we are called to more than holy work when we are clocked in. We are whole-life stewards of the blessing of God for the sake of all.

It is fitting that we ask for God's blessing in our work. We need God's wisdom, creativity, ability, sensitivity, and strength to help us succeed at what honors him. If we desire to do work that is in keeping with his character, the Spirit of God must be at the center of our lives. But God is more than a performance-enhancing drug to help us be at the top of our game. God is interested in the whole world, not just our résumé.

God also is gracious to meet us in our failures. We can lose heart at work, tire of people, live out of old wounds, feel meaningless. The blessing of God is a healing balm of affirmation that we are living meaningful lives, even if the results are not apparent.

God is the judge of our work. We need a reliable voice to assure us that we are doing our best, someone to whisper in our soul that our work is good. God is known to declare over the work of his own hands, "It is good." Why would God not do the same over ours?

God guides us in moral choices at work. The number of ethical decisions we have to make can be overwhelming. We can go soft in the daily pressure of producing results. God is the Geiger counter that clicks when we stray into unethical practices or decisions. We are called to do more than abide by the law. We are called to display the integrity of God.

God also blesses us by widening our vision to see the good being done for others in our work. Miroslav Volf tells the story of such a man.

> Some years ago at a black-tie cocktail party, I was talking to a person who introduced himself to me as a graduate of Harvard University. We were chatting, so I asked him what he did. He responded, "You will laugh when I tell you what I do," I said, "Well, try me." He replied, "I'm making urinals." I said, "Well, most men need them." And he responded, "I'm designing and producing flush-free urinals." What an extraordinary thing to do!

Water is becoming a very scarce resource, and he was helping save a lot of it, in fact some forty thousand gallons per urinal per year![2]

The vocation we are given requires the awareness of the God who called us to life and blessed us for the sake of others.

The megachurch television preacher who exchanges blessing for seed money is cheating people out of their calling. The gospel is too big to be narrowed to me and mine.

I

— 12 —

# DANCING WITH THE LAW
## SABBATH

This chapter is adapted from *Dancing with the Law: The Ten Commandments* by Dan Boone (Beacon Hill Press of Kansas City, 2010). Used by permission.

I

Remember the sabbath day, and keep it holy. Six days you shall labor and do all your work. But the seventh day is a sabbath to the LORD your God; you shall not do any work—you, your son or your daughter, your male or female slave, your livestock, or the alien resident in your towns. For in six days the LORD made heaven and earth, the sea, and all that is in them, but rested the seventh day; therefore the LORD blessed the sabbath day and consecrated it. (Exodus 20:8-11)

Everybody I know is tired. You are tired. I am tired. Your work wears on you. Your expenditure of energy in people, places, and things drains you. Your spirit is fatigued. You shoulder major responsibility. You make life-altering decisions. You hire and fire. You give counsel. You care for an elderly person. You keep an eye on a feeble neighbor. You bake a casserole for the funeral of a friend. You listen to complaining people. You hammer nails. You chase a toddler all day long and then wake up three times a night to coax him back to sleep.

In addition to the work, you battle the monotony of doing the same things repeatedly. Laundry breeds in the closet. School homework is eternal. Customers keep showing up. Things break and require fixing, again. Grass grows. Snow has to be shoveled. Reports are due by the end of the week. Little ones hit the floor, feet and mouths running. Paperwork stacks up. Planes line up on the runway. Your inbox, mailbox, and voicemail are full. Bills stack up. Groceries disappear. Gas tanks plummet toward empty.

We've done these things all our lives, every week, most days. And we grow tired of the rat race.

May I tell you one of my favorite stories?

Once upon a time the Creator created creation. As the story is told in Genesis 1, we notice a literary flow. It's hard to see unless you magnify the pattern words. Observe the pattern:

> In the beginning when God created the heavens and the earth, the earth was a formless void and darkness covered the face of the deep, while a wind from God swept over the face of the waters. Then God said, "Let there be light"; and there was light. And God saw that the light was good; and God separated the light from the darkness. God called the light Day, and the darkness he called Night. *And there was evening and there was morning, the first day.*
>
> And God said, "Let there be a dome in the midst of the waters, and let it separate the waters from the waters." So God made the dome and separated the waters that were under the dome from the waters that were above the dome. And it was so. God called the dome Sky. *And there was evening and there was morning, the second day.*

And God said, "Let the waters under the sky be gathered together into one place, and let the dry land appear." And it was so. God called the dry land Earth, and the waters that were gathered together he called Seas. And God saw that it was good. Then God said, "Let the earth put forth vegetation: plants yielding seed, and fruit trees of every kind on earth that bear fruit with the seed in it." And it was so. The earth brought forth vegetation: plants yielding seed of every kind, and trees of every kind bearing fruit with the seed in it. And God saw that it was good. *And there was evening and there was morning, the third day.*

And God said, "Let there be lights in the dome of the sky to separate the day from the night; and let them be for signs and for seasons and for days and years, and let them be lights in the dome of the sky to give light upon the earth." And it was so. God made the two great lights—the greater light to rule the day and the lesser light to rule the night—and the stars. God set them in the dome of the sky to give light upon the earth, to rule over the day and over the night, and to separate the light from the darkness. And God saw that it was good. *And there was evening and there was morning, the fourth day.*

And God said, "Let the waters bring forth swarms of living creatures, and let birds fly above the earth across the dome of the sky." So God created the great sea monsters and every living creature that moves, of every kind, with which the waters swarm, and every winged bird of every kind. And God saw that it was good. God blessed them, saying, "Be fruitful and multiply and fill the waters in the seas, and let birds multiply on the earth." *And there was evening and there was morning, the fifth day.*

And God said, "Let the earth bring forth living creatures of every kind: cattle and creeping things and wild animals of the earth of every kind." And it was so. God made the wild animals of the earth of every kind, and the cattle of every kind, and everything that creeps upon the ground of every kind. And God saw that it was good.

Then God said, "Let us make humankind in our image, according to our likeness; and let them have dominion over the fish of the sea, and over the birds of the air, and over the cattle, and over all the wild animals of the earth, and over every creeping thing that creeps upon the earth."

So God created humankind in his image, in the image of God he created them; male and female he created them. God blessed them, and God said to them, "Be fruitful and multiply, and fill the earth and subdue it; and have dominion over the fish of the sea and over the birds of the air and over every living thing that moves upon the earth." . . . And it was so. God saw everything that he had made, and indeed, it was very good. *And there was evening and there was morning, the sixth day.* (Genesis 1:1-28, 30*b*-31, emphasis added)

Do you see the pattern? Evening-morning, evening-morning, evening-morning.

Each new day begins with night. When we go to sleep, God begins the new day. We begin each day resting. While we're sawing logs, God is recalibrating his creation. The moon marks the seasons. The waves clean the shores. The lion stalks its prey. Earthworms aerate the land. Proteins repair our damaged muscles. Enzymes digest our food. Night cools the earth. Dew refreshes the ground. We wake up in a universe humming with the creative activity of God.

This cycle tells us that the world does not hinge on our work. We make our contribution late in the day. God was putting the finishing touches on creation when we were hired on day six. For all our industriousness and ingenuity, our acquisitiveness and acquiring, our competing and completing, the world does not hinge on what we do. Take us out of the picture, and life goes on.

Our corresponding fit in this evening-morning pattern is sleep-labor, sleep-labor. Interestingly, there is no biblical command to sleep. It's a pattern we can't ignore without crashing. Our bodies demand sleep. The creation story establishes a healthy pattern—evening-morning, sleep-labor.

But there's another pattern in the story:

Thus the heavens and the earth were finished, and all their multitude. And on the seventh day God finished the work that he had done, and he rested on the seventh day from all the work that he had done. So God blessed the seventh day and hallowed it, because on it God rested from all the work that he had done in creation. (Genesis 2:1-3)

After creating, God rested. God practiced Sabbath. The word *Sabbath* means stop, quit, cease and desist, rest. God stopped doing what he had been doing for six days. A new rhythm began. Six days of labor, one day of rest: 6-1, 6-1, 6-1, 6-1.

Fast-forward in time. We find ourselves in Egypt, slaves in a brick-making factory. We have a slave-driving boss. We submitted a request for a religious holiday out in the wilderness park, but the boss got ticked and figured we had too much time on our hands. Our brick quota has just been raised again. We are tired; we do the same monotonous things every day. We've been working ten hours a day, seven days a week, fifty-two weeks a year, for four hundred years. How's that for a rhythm?

And here comes God, liberating us from Pharaoh's grind and preparing us for a new career as entrepreneurs in Canaan. We stand at the foot of a smoking mountain to hear the new commands. And God says,

Remember the sabbath day, and keep it holy. Six days you shall labor and do all your work. But the seventh day is a sabbath to the LORD your God; you shall not do any work—you, your son or your daughter, your male or female slave, your livestock, or the alien resident in your towns. For in six days the LORD made heaven and earth, the sea, and all that is in them, but rested the seventh day; therefore the LORD blessed the sabbath day and consecrated it. (Exodus 20:8-11)

For the life of me, I cannot imagine any liberated slave saying, "What! No way! If I want to work seven days a week, who are you to tell me I can't? No one has the right to make me stop working!" They would have called that slave crazy. Today we call the same person a workhorse, the backbone of the company, the guts of the organization, an iron man or woman. We give that person awards and make him or her the poster child of productivity.

And there are also those people who work six days for pay, then become nonstop workers at other quests on the seventh day—white knuckling a golf club and getting more stressed with each hole, attacking the lawn with veins bulging, cleaning the house with the vengeance of germ warfare. They are restless, driven, anxious, charging—doing, doing, doing.

Barbara Brown Taylor writes:

> Someone just told me that in China, the polite answer to "How are you?" is "I am very busy, thank you." If you are very busy, then, you must be fine. If you have more to do than you can ever do, and the list never gets done, only longer, then you must be very fine, because not only in China but also right here at home, successful people are busy people. Effective people are busy people. Religious people are busy people. For millions and millions of people, busy-ness is The Way of Life.[1]

And God speaks a gift from the holy mountain: "Stop!" Are we listening?

A little later in the Exodus story, God says,

> You shall keep the sabbath, because it is holy for you; everyone who profanes it shall be put to death; whoever does any work on it shall be cut off from among the

people. Six days shall work be done, but the seventh day is a sabbath of solemn rest, holy to the LORD; whoever does any work on the sabbath day shall be put to death. Therefore the Israelites shall keep the sabbath, observing the sabbath throughout their generations, as a perpetual covenant. *It is a sign* forever between me and the people of Israel that in six days the LORD made heaven and earth, and on the seventh day he rested, and was refreshed. (Exodus 31:14-17, emphasis added)

Sabbath is a sign, a signal between God and us. When I played baseball, we had signs: fastball, curve, changeup, steal, bunt, take the next pitch. The sign existed as a way for the coach to instruct the player what to do next. To ignore the coach's sign was the quickest way to sit on the bench. In Exodus, God sends a sign to Israel. After six days' labor, God calls for a day of rest. This is somehow connected to our sanctification: "You shall keep my sabbaths, for this is a sign between me and you throughout your generations, given in order that you may know that I, the LORD, sanctify you" (Exodus 31:13). God cannot make us holy without our participation in the rhythms of grace.

There is no command to sleep, because we cannot violate the sleep-labor patterns without crashing. But we can violate the 6-1, 6-1, 6-1 pattern. Our bodies won't shut down for a while. It is physically possible to live out the pattern 7, 7, 7, 7 until we fall dead. The Jews had a name for people who did this—*slaves*.

God never intended us to live this way. God is not a slave driver. God liberates his people from slavery. We are more than the work we do. We are meant to be defined as creatures of a loving God. Work is what we are given to do in partnership with God in his creative enterprise in the world. Sabbath is part of the process. It includes meaningful, rested worship of God. In this act, we recenter our lives as a community of faith on the God who is our life. Sabbath involves family and friends. We eat together, slowly, and linger at the table to talk. We take long walks. We play together. We take naps, read novels, paint pictures, ride bikes, visit neighbors. I think the last thing God wants from us is some pious performance of avoiding life's restful joys. God is re-creating us!

As with most good gifts, we humans messed up the gift of Sabbath. This gift of Law was hamstrung with rules and regulations that made the day more about what we could not do rather than celebrating what we were invited to do. Some of Jesus' sharpest conflicts with religious leaders were over Sabbath. Don't travel on Sabbath. Don't pick grain for a snack. Don't heal the sick. The Sabbath became a burden rather than a gift. In Jesus' view, people were not made to be crammed into the Sabbath regulations; Sabbath was given as a gift of God to tired people.

If you are of a certain age and were raised in the South, then for all practical purposes the commandment might as well have read, "Remember the Sabbath day, and keep it boring." The Sabbath was the day you could not wear blue jeans, could not play ball, could not ride bikes, could not go to the movies, could not do anything but go to church in the morning and *again* at night, with a wasteland in between during which old people with little hair left on their heads but a great deal growing out of their ears sat around in rocking chairs talking about incredibly dull things, and you could not creep away for more than twelve minutes without your mother yelling, "What are you doing in there? Come back out here and visit with your Uncle Lynch and Aunt Alma, who came all the way from East Point to see you."[2]

Sabbath is permission to play like a kid. Can you dance with this law?

If you continue living at the same pace you are now, will you like the person you become in ten years? What is the quality of your life off the clock? Can you relax? Do you know how to stop working? When, during the week, does God's grace penetrate your fatigued spirit and invigorate your life? When do you get still and hear the whispering God? When do you recalibrate, recharge your soul batteries? When do you really play?

In the Christian faith, Sabbath is connected to the first day of the week, the day of resurrection. In a sense, our Sabbath is no longer the seventh day of the week, but the eighth, or the first day of the new creation. At the end of this old dying world's best effort at being God, we find a fateful Friday, a tomb-ish Saturday, and a resurrection Sunday. We are now living out the new creation begun in the resurrection of Jesus. The future becomes possible, manageable, hopeful, because Jesus is the future.

I think God hopes to catch us fully alive on Sunday,
worshipping with our whole heart,
photographing a fall tree resplendent in sunburst colors,
bouncing a snowmobile over hills,
cranking a stereo player with our favorite music and
lying on the floor singing along,
wrestling with kids in cool grass,
laughing with friends on the back porch,
running for a pass in the end zone,
curled up with a good book,
taking a nap while pretending to be interested
in a football game,
embracing the love of our life,
resting, just resting in the grace of God,
or maybe, just maybe,
dancing with the law of Sabbath.

|

— 13 —

# PARABLES ABOUT WORKERS

|

Lots of sermons about work come from the parables of Jesus in Matthew 24—25. And rightly so, because he talks about servants put in charge of their master's business, cruelty toward workers, return on investments, differing numbers of talents, bankers, and meeting human need. These parables have names like the parable of the unfaithful slave, the parable of the talents, and the judgment of the nations.

But these parables are not primarily about business practices or workplace ethics. They are about the kingdom that is dawning and who is ready to receive it and who is not. Jesus is talking about readiness for his return. Final judgment is fully in view. These parables are exposing the religious leaders who were not ready to receive the Messiah, who was right under their noses. They point to the return of the soon-to-be risen Messiah coming to earth to reign finally. These parables are clearly about being prepared.

It might be easy to chide pastors for using these parables to preach about work, since they are more about being prepared for the coming kingdom of Jesus. But we have to ask some important questions before excusing these texts from our study of work.

- Why do the eschatological parables borrow so much from the world of work?
- Why are they so interested in the accountable relationship between slaves and masters, employers and employees?
- Why is the chief currency of these parables money, labor, and return on investment?
- Is it possible that work done Christianly is the best snapshot of a life lived in right relationship with God?
- Is the faithful servant in these parables the one who understood that he was working in partnership with God all along and kept the concerns of the master foremost in his daily decisions?

Let's take a look at the parables.

## The Faithful or the Unfaithful Slave

Who then is the faithful and wise slave, whom his master has put in charge of his household, to give the other slaves their allowance of food at the proper time? Blessed is that slave whom his master will find at work when he arrives. Truly I tell you, he will put that one in charge of all his possessions. But if that wicked slave says to himself, "My master is delayed," and he begins to beat his fellow slaves, and eats and drinks with drunkards, the master of the slave will come on a day when he does not expect him and at an hour he does not know. He will cut him in pieces and put him with the hypocrites, where there will be weeping and gnashing of teeth. (Matthew 24:45-51)

Two interpretations of this parable are possible, and both may be right.

- Jesus may be talking about Israel, given work to do by the Father. Yet she was consumed by nationalistic interests and economic desires, failing to attend to the master's business. When Jesus appears, God will surprise the unprepared servant who assumed no one was watching. This is a dereliction of duty. Israel is declared a hypocrite, because she has been posing as God's servant while mistreating her neighbor and indulging herself. If this interpretation is correct, the religious leaders are under frontal attack from the parable of Jesus and mad enough to kill him, which comes a few chapters later.
- The other interpretation is that Jesus is telling this parable to his disciples as he stands on the Mount of Olives describing the coming of the kingdom. He is going away for a while but will return at an unannounced time to make all things new. He is leaving his disciples to work until he returns. Their work depicts the kingdom that is coming. It involves righteous treatment of others and diligent focus on the activity of God. When Jesus returns, those who have been working for his cause will be given charge of all creation. Those who have been selfish, lazy, and unethical will take their place among hypocrites who, according to Wisdom literature, end up crying and gnashing their teeth in hopes of a bite to eat.

These two interpretations are also connected to the Wisdom literature of Proverbs. They portray two kinds of servants—the wise and the fool. The wise person is prepared, diligent, accountable, productive, and ready. The fool is lazy, inattentive, and a slacker. The surprise return of Jesus is not so much meant to catch the fool as to reveal the fool for what he or she has been all along.

Lessons for the workplace in this parable are plentiful.

1. The kind of work we do when no one is looking is a key determinant of our character.

2. How we steward the authority/possessions entrusted to us is a measure of our respect for those who trust us. It is also a revelation of our respect for those over whom we have been given authority.
3. We will answer for what we do, now or later.
4. How power gets used in the workplace is an ethical issue for which there should be accountability.
5. Work should be given the focus and attention it deserves.
6. God has expectations about our work.

While these texts are primarily about the work of the kingdom, they are applicable to our daily jobs, because the kingdom of God is all-consuming. There is not one square inch of all creation over which God does not say, "This is mine." God is not interested in our religious life; God is interested in our whole life. The fact that these parables reference the work relationship is a strong signal that God is being served in our places of employment.

What might this parable look like today?

Perry Bigelow is a Chicago homebuilder. He has built his company on Christian ethics and practices. His company policy is "We will never knowingly lie to each other, a home purchaser, a supplier or subcontractor, or government official. We place a high premium on personal integrity." His homes are designed with large front porches and extra-wide sidewalks to invite community formation. His homes are also energy efficient in respect for stewardship of the environment and its limited resources. Each housing development contains low, medium, and higher-priced houses to demographic diversity. Perry Bigelow has brought joy to his customers—many of them first-time homebuyers, many of them working families needing a safe, neighborly, affordable community to live in. He has also blessed the city of Aurora by building a subdivision that contributes to the local tax base, generating revenue for schools and municipal services. And he has blessed future generations by taking the biblical value of sustainability seriously enough to let it shape his product design.[1]

This is the kind of servant that the master will find doing his business when he returns. Perry probably doesn't spend his days watching the eastern sky for a messianic descent or reading predictions of the date of the end of the world. If Jesus returns tomorrow, he'll probably find Perry hunched over a set of blueprints with the needs of people in mind.

## The Parable of the Talents

It's also like a man going off on an extended trip. He called his servants together and delegated responsibilities. To one he gave five thousand dollars, to another two thousand, to a third one thousand, depending on their abilities. Then he left. Right off, the first servant went to work and doubled his master's investment. The second did the same. But the man with the single thousand dug a hole and carefully buried his master's money. After a long absence, the master of those three servants came back and settled up with them. The one given five thousand dollars showed him how he had doubled his investment. His master commended him: "Good work! You did your job well. From now on be my partner." The servant with the two thousand showed how he also had doubled his master's investment. His master commended him: "Good work! You did your job well. From now on be my partner." The servant given one thousand said, "Master, I know you have high standards and hate careless ways, that you demand the best and make no allowances for error. I was afraid I might disappoint you, so I found a good hiding place and secured your money. Here it is, safe and sound down to the last cent." The master was furious. "That's a terrible way to live! It's criminal to live cautiously like that! If you knew I was after the best, why did you do less than the least? The least you could have done would have been to invest the sum with the bankers, where at least I would have gotten a little interest. Take the thousand and give it to the one who risked the most. And get rid of this 'play-it-safe' who won't go out on a limb. Throw him out into utter darkness." (Matthew 25:14-30, TM)

The same two interpretations possible in the preceding parable are also possible here.

- Jesus could have been speaking to Israel, covenanted with God and entrusted with the Law and expected to be a light to the nations. Israel failed to invest that which was given her and was now under judgment.
- Or the parable could have been instruction to the disciples that they had been called to the work of the kingdom, entrusted with the story of Jesus, and sent into the world to bear fruit. Either way, servants are expected to produce results from what they have been given.

A talent in this parable and in biblical times was not something we are good at doing. It was a large sum of money equivalent to what a person would earn over fifteen years. The servants in the parable did not have this kind of money nor would they ever by their own labor. They have been in the service of a wealthy master and have earned his trust at three different levels. No doubt, their prior performance has caused the master to entrust to them amounts in keeping with their performance. To the top performer he entrusts the most, to the lowest the least.

The master's confidence in the first two servants proves justified. They are congratulated and given more responsibility. The third servant is an utter failure, not because he is not a good businessman, but because he did not even try. His own response condemns him. He knew what his master wanted—return on the investment, and he did not even try.

He did not open an interest-bearing account, he did not loan it out to another for interest. He did nothing in keeping with who he knew his master to be or what his master wanted. By taking no risk, he assured himself of the master's displeasure.

The parable compares the business of life in the service of God to the business of commerce. It compares the use of all God has given one—not just specific "talents," but all that one has and is—in God's service, with the use of a financial loan in order to make a financial profit for the investor. The reason the master is furious with the third slave is that, for a businessman, the whole point of money is to be used and spent and circulated to make more money. Money merely hoarded might as well just be thrown away. In the same way, what God has given us—ourselves, our lives, our faith, our abilities, our gifts, our possessions—is given in order to be spent and put into circulation. Our lives are to be expended in God's service, becoming thereby the source of further blessing for others and for ourselves. Only in that sense is God like the rapacious investor interested only in profit.[2]

The same connections to Wisdom literature are found in this parable where we see the difference between the wise one who invests and the fool whose laziness keeps him from doing anything. Sitting on assets is never enough. Saying a prayer of salvation and then living a life without risk is not enough. Protecting ourselves from the big bad sin-wolf is not enough. Doing nothing here on earth, while waiting for heaven to pick us up on the glory train, is not enough. God has entrusted us with kingdom life, which is to be risked in the world in hopes of being the light that dawns on those who live in darkness.

Lest this begins to sound like merit-based salvation, it is important to note that good works (return on investments) is not what gets us eternal life. We have already been given eternal life as the gracious entrustment of the Father. This is about how life is meant to be lived—not in protection mode but in an aggressive partnership with God in the middle of the world. Burying what we have been given suggests that we neither know the Giver nor appreciate the gift. Saying yes to God comes with all kinds of strings attached.

Lessons for the way we do our daily work abound.

1. We are always the recipient of all that we have, never the owner. It all goes back in the box at the end. God is owner; we are stewards.

2. We are not accountable for what we have not been given but are to be effective with what we have been given.

3. God expects results from his investment in us and has made it clear that we will answer for our lives.

4. While we may be called to take risks, the only certain way that we will fail is to not even try. Those who lose their life for God's sake, will find it.

5. The more we succeed in using what we have been given, the more will be entrusted to us. Good work invites the opportunity to do more good work.

6. We can please God by our effective work if it is in keeping with his interests in the world. Our responsible initiative puts a smile on the face of God.

While the world divides the sacred from the secular, the church from the workplace, nothing could be further from the truth. The essence of the kingdom of God is seen in the workplace. We are entrusted with the opportunity to produce. We go about our work as wise ones. The character of God can be discerned from the way we work as precisely as from any other human venue. People see our God in the way we work. That's why our discipleship is played out every time we clock in.

|

— 14 —

# WORK THAT WILL LAST

|

As a college president, I find myself talking to people about gifts to the university. When people begin to contemplate the day they will no longer be drawing breath, they begin to think about letting go of their accumulated goods. As the old preacher says, a hearse is seldom accompanied to the cemetery by a U-Haul. We don't take it with us.

One of the questions I find myself asking these reflective stewards of goods is this: How do you want to be remembered?

Some people go so far as to write their obituary or funeral eulogy. This tells us that some kind of eternal seed is planted in our being. We believe that what we have done will follow us into the future in some way. I suggest that the crowning act of our devotion to God may be the witness we leave behind by our gifts that support God's work in the world after we are gone.

What better way than to invest in a Christian college education for young servants of God? This is a gift that has a lifetime return as a skilled servant wakes up every morning to do God's work in the world. Okay. There. I made the presidential pitch for endowed scholarships. That's my work, you know.

As people of the resurrection, we have affirmed in the Apostles' Creed that we believe in the resurrection of the dead. Our last breath is not our final moment of consciousness. We will be raised into the future of God's tomorrow. But what of the work we do in our bodies while we occupy earth as its responsible caretakers? Will it last? Was it there only to occupy us? Was it like a resistant weight that developed our spiritual muscles by requiring us to lift it again and again over a lifetime? Was it God's evangelistic strategy of putting us shoulder to shoulder with our pagan neighbors? Was it a testing ground for our witness? Does our work have any value other than its incidental contribution to the fiber of our character?

Paul seems to think that our work is so important to God that it will be tested in the judgment. "For all of us must appear before the judgment seat of Christ, so that each may receive recompense for what has been in the body, whether good or evil" (2 Corinthians 5:10).

In purely economic terms, we have one more job evaluation and one more payday coming beyond the grave. It matters to God what we do.

It would be easy to slide into an earned salvation here. If God gives us the passing grade on our work, we get to go to heaven. Otherwise we stoke fires forever. This is not what is being suggested by me or Paul. What is being evaluated is not our relationship with God but what we have done in this relationship. What did our life produce?

I know this raises lots of questions. Will Billy Graham get a bigger bonus or bigger mansion because he has been so prolific in his service of God? Or maybe Mother Teresa. Will some of us get a lump of coal because we were bad boys and girls and squandered our opportunities to do great work for God in the workplace? Will there be a pecking order in heaven? Will martyrs finally get their due reward? Will the single mother who sacrificed for three children, worked countless hours, and got no thanks be fully vested in heaven's retirement plan? Will her ungrateful churched children have to wait on her hand and foot for eternity? Sounds like a fair deal to me.

I don't know. But I do know that Paul is on to something as he writes about the importance of our work on earth as having eternal value. The best hint of this is found in 1 Corinthians 3:

> But for right now, friends, I'm completely frustrated by your unspiritual dealings with each other and with God. You're acting like infants in relation to Christ, capable of nothing much more than nursing at the breast. Well, then, I'll nurse you since you don't seem capable of anything more. As long as you grab for what makes you feel good or makes you look important, are you really much different than a babe at the breast, content only when everything's going your way? When one of you says, "I'm on Paul's side," and another says, "I'm for Apollos," aren't you being totally infantile? Who do you think Paul is, anyway? Or Apollos, for that matter? Servants, both of us—servants who waited on you as you gradually learned to entrust your lives to our mutual Master. We each carried out our servant assignment. I planted the seed, Apollos watered the plants, but God made you grow. It's not the one who plants or the one who waters who is at the center of this process but God, who makes things grow. Planting and watering are menial servant jobs at minimum wages. What makes them worth doing is the God we are serving. You happen to be God's field in which we are working. Or, to put it another way, you are God's house. Using the gift God gave me as a good architect, I designed blueprints; Apollos is putting up the walls. Let each carpenter who comes on the job take care

to build on the foundation! Remember, there is only one foundation, the one already laid: Jesus Christ. Take particular care in picking out your building materials. Eventually there is going to be an inspection. If you use cheap or inferior materials, you'll be found out. The inspection will be thorough and rigorous. You won't get by with a thing. If your work passes inspection, fine; if it doesn't, your part of the building will be torn out and started over. But *you* won't be torn out; you'll survive—but just barely. You realize, don't you, that you are the temple of God, and God himself is present in you? No one will get by with vandalizing God's temple, you can be sure of that. God's temple is sacred—and you, remember, *are* the temple. Don't fool yourself. Don't think that you can be wise merely by being up-to-date with the times. Be God's fool—that's the path to true wisdom. What the world calls smart, God calls stupid. It's written in Scripture, He exposes the chicanery of the chic. The Master sees through the smoke screens of the know-it-alls. I don't want to hear any of you bragging about yourself or anyone else. Everything is already yours as a gift—Paul, Apollos, Peter, the world, life, death, the present, the future—all of it is yours, and you are privileged to be in union with Christ, who is in union with God. (1 Corinthians 3, TM)

While the primary reference of this text is to the work of establishing the church, we find Paul using, similar to Matthew in the parables, examples of common labor to make the point. The two dominant images are farming and construction. Again, the activity of God in the world is best pictured in the work we do. And while this text is not written as an appendage to a topical sermon on work, its application is most fitting.

Here's the problem in Corinth. Groupies had formed around different church leaders, championing their key role in building the church. Each group had its star apostle—Peter, Apollos, Paul. Allegiance to one over the others had created a division in the church. Rather than being unified under the same God who was at work in each apostle, the church was fractured. Paul makes it clear that each apostle played a role in the garden of God—planting, watering, pruning, harvesting—but it was God who grew the garden. The work of the people of God is not meant to be pitted against that of others but is part of the whole. And the work of God that Paul is referring to is the establishment of a people who are viewed as a temple being built for God to dwell in. Lots of people work in the garden, and they work as co-workers with God, doing different tasks. But the growth of the garden is the handiwork of God.

In this light, it is interesting to note that God clocks in too. While God calls us to our work and gifts us for the work, God also works alongside us. Because God is working, we are fruitful. The image of a God who rolls up his sleeves and gets down in the dirt with us co-workers brings God to the daily worksite. Our theology of the presence of God called the Holy Spirit suggests that God is as near as the breath we breathe. And as we work, God is growing something. In 1 Corinthians 3, a church. In your workplace, a healing office where people enter sick and leave in health. Or a road that cannot be safely ridden until you fill the potholes. Or a classroom where necessary knowledge is imparted. You may be planting the seed and someone else may come along later and water it, but God is making something good happen.

Because we are often unaware of the presence of God in the workplace, we are prone to think we are making things grow all by our little selves. Look what I did! To be enamored with our work apart from our partnership with God is to be pumped full of pride. Paul calls that "fleshy." Successful people often regale anyone who is willing to listen with their story of what this place was like before I got here and what it is like now. It is a litany of ego littered with human accomplishments that may all be well and good. Half of what they say may even be true. But if they have failed to recognize their co-worker, God, they have created something that will not stand the test of time or the final judgment.

To speak about this, Paul changes metaphors—from farming to construction. There is only one foundation that good work can be built upon. It is the foundation that has already been laid—the life, death, and resurrection of Jesus. Anything else is sinking sand, shoddy concrete, unsquare foundation, unlevel floor. Its very base is off-center, and regardless of the impressive structure that rises to crown the human effort, it will not stand. Why? Because it is not founded on the activity of the God who raised Jesus from the dead. This crooked old foundation is still part of the world that is dying, not the world that is being renewed.

Good work is grounded in Jesus and his purposes in the world. It begins there and ends there. Does this mean that sinful people cannot do good work? No. God's grace has been poured out on the world, and many are participating in good work without knowledge of the God who enables them. It is called prevenient grace—the grace that precedes salvation. I know non-Christians who are doing good justice work. I know people who have turned their back on the church because of the shoddy thinking and living of the people of God and are doing outstanding work in the political field—not even realizing that God is at work through them. Similar to Cyrus the Persian in Isaiah, God has worked through many an unsuspecting creature to accomplish his purposes. But this does not change the reality of Paul's point. Those who walk with God are co-workers with God, building on the foundation that has been laid in Jesus, and we should expect to give account for our work.

Paul also suggests that the choice of building material is critical to the venture. Cheap, inferior materials will not stand the test of judgment. He lists several possibilities—gold, silver, precious stones, wood, hay, straw. The day of the Lord will test everything with fire, the metaphor of God's sweeping examination. Fire will expose all things, clearing away that which cannot withstand the heat of judgment. Those who build with gold, silver, and precious stones will find their work standing, while those who have chosen inferior materials will be left standing in a pile of ashes.

If this is to be the case with our work, what are the qualities of work that will stand the test of judgment?

- The work is done in partnership with God, in humble awareness that God is at work in the world and has invited us to join him in the workplace. It is an act of worshipful response to the God who offered us such meaningful partnership. Helen Keller said, "I long to accomplish great and noble tasks, but it is my chief duty to accomplish humble tasks as though they were great and noble. The world is moved along, not only by the mighty shoves of its heroes, but also by the aggregate of the tiny pushes of each honest worker."[1]

- It is built on the foundation that is laid in the story of Jesus. The work is of the nature and character of Jesus, the full expression of what it means to be human. "Your task is to find the symbolic ways of doing things differently, planting flags in hostile soil, setting up signposts that say there is a different way to be human."[2]

- It is for the common good. It meets human need and fulfills the command to love the neighbor, care for the stranger, and help the weak.

- It is in some way an answer to the Lord's Prayer—"Thy kingdom come. Thy will be done in earth, as it is in heaven" (Matthew 6:10, KJV). It is not enough to be ethical, professional, and fair. We are called to be the signal of a radical new reign breaking into human existence, defeating the powers of darkness that dehumanize and offering blessing for the good of all.

- It creates peaceful, just community. God's creatures are given place and space to live together in ways that allow humans to thrive in joy and justice.
- It stewards the earth and its resources, looking unselfishly to the needs of future generations. If our work views the planet as expendable, a floating ball in the cosmic sea waiting to be fried to a crisp, we have missed the signal that the future home of God will be among us. Jesus hears the groaning earth and comes to reign by making all things new.
- It will reflect the ways of wisdom and not the ways of the foolish.

Paul's letter to the Corinthians opens a window to an eschatological understanding of work. His image of our work as *gardeners* points back to Eden in Genesis 1; and his image of our work as *builders* points forward to the Holy City of Revelation 20—21. Our work will be judged. What has been done in Christ will last. We will be rewarded for work that is pleasing in the sight of God.

Of all the paydays we've ever experienced, this is the one that matters most.

|

— 15 —

# WHEN WORK MESSES WITH CHURCH RELATIONSHIPS

|

The choir director of this small North Carolina church owned the local furniture factory. He also served on the board and was chair of the finance committee. Over several years he had employed members of the congregation to work in his factory. A generous man with a soft heart, he was willing to give many congregants a chance at employment who otherwise would not have gotten past the human resources office. The church people viewed him as a protective father figure. In the workplace, they curried favor with him in hopes of promotions and raises. In the church, they sang in his choir, promoted his election to the governing board, and volunteered for any cause that he became associated with. The pastor of the church knew that any issue of substance that came before the congregation for a vote would most likely be decided by the factory owner. Like children behind the Pied Piper, they would march in step. While this man never sought a power block in the church, he had it as the result of his economic power in the lives of people.

Imagine the scenario when the board votes to relocate the church and the factory owner opposes the move; or when a new pastor is to be selected and the female candidate is, well, female—to the distaste of the factory owner. How will he use his power? What will the factory workers do? Vote with him or vote according to what seems best for the mission of the church? Dare they oppose him at the possible cost of a job or promotion? And how does a pastor lead in this situation? Does he risk losing the primary financial base of the church over the minority preference of one powerful board member, or does he demonstrate his loyalty to the mission of God by leading toward the future that seems right for the church?

When work relationships bring power structures into the church, it can get messy.

That's what was happening in Thessalonica. Paul addressed the issue the first time in 1 Thessalonians 4:9-12.

Now concerning love of the brothers and sisters, you do not need to have anyone write to you, for you yourselves have been taught by God to love one another; and indeed you do love all the brothers and sisters throughout Macedonia. But we urge you, beloved, to do so more and more, to aspire to live quietly, to mind your own affairs, and to work with your hands, as we directed you, so that you may behave properly toward outsiders and be dependent on no one.

In the Gentile world of Thessalonica, it was common for people to attach themselves to wealthy patrons or benefactors. In the Greco-Roman world, life was structured by a complex set of relationships between patrons and their beneficiaries. The wealthy benefitted the less wealthy with financial assistance to provide them a living. Andy Johnson writes about the dependence of the client on the benefactor and the reciprocal expectation that the client would publicly speak out in support of his benefactor's economic and social interests. The client would make a public display of honoring the patron. But it did not end there. These same patrons were the beneficiaries of even higher status patrons. It was a totem pole of social ranking with each level being served by those below and serving those above. At the top of the totem pole was the emperor. This was the way of life in Thessalonica.[1]

Three problems were evident in these client/patron relationships. First, given the nature of the church as brothers and sisters in Christ standing on equal ground at the foot of the cross, any ranking of social importance is an affront to the family of faith. The Christian call to service does not imagine any ranking of those serving or being served. We serve one another. The very nature of the hierarchical economic relationships betrays the unity of the church. Especially when we come to the Lord's Table there is to be no distinction among us. We are one at the table with our Lord.

The second problem concerns our likeness to Jesus. He disavowed status as the Son of God and humbled himself in service to the outcast. If the members of the church measured social standing as the prerequisite to service, there would be no one to serve the needy among them. By being dependent on the wealthier ones, those with less would not be working with their hands in order that they might have something to share with the needy. Johnson writes,

> For an able-bodied church member to attempt to cultivate a client relationship with another member of the church as their patron in lieu of engaging in some form of labor would lessen the ability of the church to take care of its genuinely "weak" members. It would also impede its ability to continue being a channel of grace (especially in the form of economic aid) to other Christians outside Thessalonica. Such a life pattern would stand in tension with that of the cruciform Lord.[2]

Paul consistently called the Thessalonians to adopt the ways of Jesus even as he had. In 1 Thessalonians 2:9-10, he reminded them of his example. "You remember our labor and toil, brothers and sisters; we worked night and day, so that we might not burden any of you while we proclaimed to you the gospel of God. You are witnesses, and God also, how pure, upright, and blameless our conduct was toward you."

This was Paul's model as a tentmaker among them. Refusing to burden them with his needs, he worked hard and long that the gospel might be given freely. While it was his right to expect their support, he refused to do so. Johnson writes, "He did this with only their benefit in mind demanding no reciprocal response from them as the logic of the patronage system might have dictated."[3]

The third problem confronting the church in the client/patron relationship was the issue of primary loyalty. Paul is concerned about their relationship "to those outside" the church. Should members of the church align themselves with a patron who was not a follower of Jesus? Would the loyalty of these believers be compromised by the expectations of the pagan patron? The gospel of Jesus called for a radical break with the dying ways of the old world. Paul articulated the new cruciform behavior consistently in dealing with ethical issues. He had just called the men of Thessalonica to control their bodies in sexual behavior that fit the pattern of respect and love demonstrated by Jesus. Paul and the apostles had modeled such a life, rather than the life of sexual liberty championed in Greco-Roman culture. Now he calls for economic relationships that are in keeping with the way of Jesus. By full devotion to Christ as Lord, the Christian was free from all competing obligations, dependent on no one, a productive wage-earner in the congregation, and a person of resource capable of loving the brother or sister in need with tangible aid.

Apparently, Paul's wisdom went unheeded. He returned to the topic in his second letter to the Thessalonians, only this time with a pointed response for the church. He wrote:

Now we command you, beloved,
in the name of our Lord Jesus Christ,
to keep away from believers
who are living in idleness
and not according to the tradition
that they received from us.
For you yourselves know how you ought to imitate us;
we were not idle when we were with you,
and we did not eat anyone's bread without paying for it;
but with toil and labor we worked night and day,
so that we might not burden any of you.
This was not because we do not have that right,
but in order to give you an example to imitate.
For even when we were with you,
we gave you this command:
Anyone unwilling to work should not eat.
For we hear that some of you are living in idleness,
mere busybodies, not doing any work.
Now such persons we command and exhort
in the Lord Jesus Christ
to do their work quietly and to earn their own living.
Brothers and sisters,
do not be weary in doing what is right.
Take note of those who do not obey
what we say in this letter;
have nothing to do with them,
so that they may be ashamed.
Do not regard them as enemies,
but warn them as believers.
Now may the Lord of peace himself
give you peace at all times in all ways.
The Lord be with all of you.
(2 Thessalonians 3:6-16)
Some were refusing to work with their own hands, pre-
ferring a life of dependence on others. Paul used stronger

terms for these believers than in his first letter. He suggests they are living in "disorderly idleness," eating bread someone else worked for, and using their idle time as busybodies. His recommendations are stern. If this person refuses to work, he should not eat. Nor should they take pity on him and provide food. They should separate from him, disinviting him to their gatherings and the Lord's Table. Paul also intimates that these idlers were a burden to the community, something Paul was most careful to avoid.

It is clear that Paul is speaking of the treatment of a brother or sister, not someone outside the community of faith. And he is not calling for this reaction to a momentary stint of laziness but to a way of life that rejects work in favor of dependence on others.

Johnson writes,

> In this respect, it was crucial for Paul and his co-senders to model the pattern of life among them that was worthy of the kingdom into which they were being called, the cruciform life pattern, which had characterized the one whose royal coming would consummate that kingdom.
>
> . . . In negative terms, that pattern of life entailed not living in disorderly idleness or eating bread from anyone without paying for it. In positive terms, it entailed engaging in burdensome, low status activity requiring exertion and hardship in order not to burden others in the community.
>
> . . . Not only did they embody this life pattern among the Thessalonians, Paul says that he and his companions commanded the audience over and over when they were with them "if anyone is not willing to continue working, don't let them keep eating." Whatever the detailed social background is to such a statement and the situation it assumes, it is clear that while he was in Thessalonica, Paul was aware of some who were a part of the community whose life pattern was anything but cruciform. By refus-

ing to work, they became a burden to their brothers and sisters either by receiving free individual handouts of food from them; by eating with them at common meals without ever contributing anything; or perhaps by both of the above. In any case, while Paul seeks to inculcate cruciform behavior between community members, he will not tolerate some members who profess allegiance to the Crucified One using the costly self-giving actions of others simply to further their own advantage. This sort of behavior is the opposite of the cruciform pattern of activity through which God is at work to sanctify the community.[4]

As always, discipline is never the final word or intent. The aim is a life that honors God. By confronting the idlers in this way, it is Paul's hope to restore them to the church as mature followers of Jesus, whose work ethic reflects that of the Lord. To love the brother is to take the steps necessary to move him from a life of folly to wisdom. Paul demonstrates such love for the Thessalonians. "As you know, we dealt with each one of you like a father with his children, urging and encouraging you and pleading that you lead a life worthy of God, who calls you into his own kingdom and glory" (1 Thessalonians 2:11-12). The ultimate goal of such discipline is true witness to the way of Jesus and peace in the community.

What might it look like for the church to take this teaching into account?

I suggest that it might challenge the nature of some of our compassionate ministries. When our aid to the needy causes them to settle into a life of dependence rather than seeking to provide for themselves, we are failing to love them in the way Paul describes love. And when we fail to call them to contribute to the needs of others, we are allowing them to belong to the church with a lower calling. Paul urged the Ephesians to "labor and work honestly with their own hands, so as to have something to share with the needy" (Ephesians 4:28b).

For the church to preach this gospel would move people from dependencies on charities and governments toward gainful employment. It would also add to the dignity of the person who is weaned from a life of dependence. But we must tread carefully here. This maturing journey from dependence to productivity calls for friendship, truth, and help. It is not enough to publicly deride the needy from the pulpit as idlers. If we love them, we must help them find and develop their skills, seek employment, and coach them in their work. We must also recognize that some among us are not capable of work due to illness, incapacities, or life situations. These are our brothers and sisters. We will offer them not only our aid, but also human dignity, in the way we offer help.

A few years ago, President George H. W. Bush called on the churches of America to make a dent in poverty. His challenge was that every church, synagogue, and mosque in America would identify two homeless people and work to move them toward employment, shelter, and community. I believe this is a valid call. Sadly, the challenge fell on deaf ears. As a nation wrestling with economic viability, I have often wondered what it would be like if the church of Jesus took this call seriously and moved thousands, if not millions, from a life of dependence to a life of sharing.

The Thessalonian correspondence also warns us that economic relationships within the church need careful scrutiny. It is to be expected that church members will often work with and for each other, compete for business with each other, and provide jobs for each other. Our text is not a call to a formal legalism that forbids such connections, but it is a warning that these relationships need wise counsel and discernment. The bank president and the bank janitor sit on the same pew as brothers, drinking from the same cup and breaking the same bread. Our primary identity in this world is our unity in Jesus.

|

— 16 —

# WHEN WE ALL
# GET TO HEAVEN

|

My early views of heaven were out of this world, off this planet, and disconnected from most of what we know as culture and daily life. Heaven was the place we would be whisked off to at the return of Jesus. The rapture would rupture time and we would find ourselves floating into the heavens to a place we had never set foot on before. Not anymore.

My study of the Old Testament prophets, the teaching of Jesus about the kingdom of God, the groaning earth of Romans 8:18-25, and the Revelation of Jesus to John have given me a very different picture of the coming kingdom. According to the prophets, most of the characteristics of the Day of the Lord are earthy. According to Romans 8, the groaning earth will experience the same resurrection as our dead bodies. And according to the Revelation, the coming kingdom is a city coming down to earth, not the Flying Nun and her pals winging their way into the skies.[1]

Then I saw a new heaven and a new earth; for the first heaven and the first earth had passed away, and the sea was no more. And I saw the holy city, the new Jerusalem, coming down out of heaven from God, prepared as a bride adorned for her husband. And I heard a loud voice from the throne saying, "See, the home of God is among mortals. He will dwell with them; they will be his peoples, and God himself will be with them; he will wipe every tear from their eyes. Death will be no more; mourning and crying and pain will be no more, for the first things have passed away." And the one who was seated on the throne said, "See, I am making all things new." Also he said, "Write this, for these words are trustworthy and true." (Revelation 21:1-5)

I am not saying that heaven is this old earth under the conquest of Jesus. But I am suggesting that God intends to redeem this earth even as he intends to redeem our decaying bodies. It does not say that God will make "all new things" but that God will "make all things new." What sin, death, and darkness have ruined, God will restore. Nor am I saying that this earth is all there is to heaven. Our planet will belong to the whole redeemed order of creation, including the galaxies.

Two texts in the Revelation of Jesus to John intrigue me in their relation to the work we do.

And I heard a voice from heaven saying, "Write this: Blessed are the dead who from now on die in the Lord." "Yes," says the Spirit, "they will rest from their labors, for their deeds follow them." (Revelation 14:13)

While it is apparent from the context that the labors mentioned refer to the suffering that these saints have endured under the dark powers of the Roman Empire, it is also to be noted that our deeds follow us. Similar to 1 Corinthians 3 and dissimilar to Ecclesiastes, our work does not disappear like a morning fog. It follows us. God preserves what we do, not only as a witness to how we have lived, but also as something whose value is not extinguished.

This thought is carried further in Revelation 21 where the holy city, the New Jerusalem, is being described. Near the end of the description we find a surprise.

And the city has no need of sun or moon to shine on it, for the glory of God is its light, and its lamp is the Lamb. The nations will walk by its light, and the kings of the earth will bring their glory into it. Its gates will never be shut by day—and there will be no night there. People will bring into it the glory and the honor of the nations. (Revelation 21:23-26)

These kings of the earth have, throughout the Revelation, resisted the claims of God and served the evil beast. They met their demise at the dethroning of the Great Prostitute in Revelation 18:21-24. We thought we were done with them. Yet here, in keeping with the hopes of the Old Testament prophets, they become part of a long line streaming to the holy city of God to honor God. And what they bring with them is their labor, work, and culture as a gift that honors God. Even work that is done outside of a relationship with God becomes a recognition of the Lordship of Jesus. God redeems everything!

Andy Crouch asks:

Are we creating and cultivating things that have a chance of furnishing the New Jerusalem? Will the cultural goods we devote our lives to—the food we cook and consume, the music we purchase and practice, the movies we watch and make, the enterprises we earn our paychecks from and invest our wealth in—be identified as the glory and honor of our cultural tradition? Or will they be remembered as mediocrities at best, dead ends at worst? . . . Clearly some of the cultural goods found in the New Jerusalem will have been created and cultivated by people who may well not accept the Lamb's invitation. . . . Yet the best of their work may survive. Can that be said of the goods we are devoting our lives to?

. . . This is, it seems to me, a standard for cultural responsibility that is both more demanding and more liberating than the way we Christians often gauge our work's significance. We tend to have altogether too short a time frame for the worth of our work. We ask if this book will be noticed, this store will have a profitable quarter, this contract will be accepted. Some of these are useful intermediate steps for assessing whether our cultural work is of lasting value, but our short-term evaluations can be misleading if our work is not also held up to the long horizon of God's redemptive purpose. On the other hand, knowing that the New Jerusalem will be furnished with the best of every culture frees us from having to give a "religious" or evangelistic explanation for everything we do. We are free simply to make the best we can of the world, in concert with our forebearers and our neighbors.[2]

One day, all good work will be laid at the feet of the One who called us to it as an act of honor. We call that worship.

Work is found in our biblical story from beginning to end. We first clock in in a garden. We are caretakers, stewards, and co-workers with God. We are redeemed from our failed corporate takeover of Eden and offered the opportunity to envision the coming kingdom. As co-laborers with our elder brother, Jesus, we clock in for work that will last. We become a sign of the city of God. And our last act of devotion is to lay all that we have done at his feet in an act of worship.

When Christians clock in, something good is going on.

P.S. I bought a riding lawn mower the other day so I could pull my grandkids in a cart behind it. I discovered that mowing is easier without pushing. Old dogs can learn new tricks. . . . which gives me hope for us all.

# NOTES

## Chapter 1

1. Merle Travis. "Sixteen Tons." Copyright © 1947 Unichappell Music Inc. and Elvis Presley Music.

2. Dolly Parton. "Nine to Five." Copyright © 1980 VELVET APPLE MUSIC and WARNER-TAMERLANE PUBLISHING CORP.

3. David Allan Coe. "Take This Job and Shove It." Copyright © 1977 WARNER-TAMERLANE PUBLISHING CORP.

## Chapter 2

1. David McKenna, *Love Your Work: Your Daily Work Can Be a Great Spiritual Resource* (Wheaton, Ill.: Victor Books, 1990).

## Chapter 3

1. Lester DeKoster, *Work: The Meaning of Your Life* (Grand Rapids: Christian's Library Press, 2010), 1-9.

2. Ben Witherington III, *Work: A Kingdom Perspective on Labor* (Grand Rapids: William B. Eerdmans, 2011).

3. Miroslav Volf, *Work in the Spirit: Toward a Theology of Work* (Eugene, Oreg.: Wipf and Stock Publishers, 1991), 71-79.

4. Dietrich Bonhoeffer, *Ethics*, vol. 6 of *Works* (Minneapolis: Fortress Press, 2005), 289-97.

5. Frederick Buechner, *Wishful Thinking: A Seeker's ABC* (San Francisco: Harper, 1993), 119.

6. Dorothy Sayers, "Why Work?" in *Creed or Chaos?* (London: Methuen & Co., 1947), 47-64.

7. N. T. Wright, *The Challenge of Jesus* (Downers Grove, Ill.: IVP Academic Press, 1999), 174-97.

8. Barbara Brown Taylor, *An Altar in the World: A Geography of Faith* (New York: Harper One, 2009), 119.

9. Ibid., 120.

## Chapter 4

1. Stephen R. Covey, *The 7 Habits of Highly Effective People: Powerful Lessons in Personal Change* (New York: Free Press, Simon & Schuster, Inc., 1989).

## Chapter 6

1. Barbara Brown Taylor, *Gospel Medicine* (Boston: Cowley Publications, 1995), 160.

## Chapter 7

1. Eugene Peterson, *The Message: The Bible in Contemporary Language* (Carol Stream, Ill.: NavPress, 2002), 829.

2. Derek Kidner, *Proverbs* (Downers Grove, Ill.: InterVarsity Press, 1964), 42-43.

## Chapter 8

1. Cornelius Plantinga, Jr., *Not the Way It's Supposed to Be: A Breviary of Sin* (Grand Rapids: Eerdmans, 1996), 195.

2. Ibid., 196-97.

## Chapter 10

1. See Dan Boone, *The Worship Plot: Finding Unity in Our Common Story* (Kansas City: Beacon Hill Press of Kansas City, 2007). This book suggests a five-move plotted worship experience: entrance, bad news, good news, response of the people, blessing.

2. Martin Luther King, Jr., *Letter from Birmingham Jail* (Washington, D.C.: Trinity Forum Reading, 2012), 14.

3. Wright, *Challenge of Jesus*, 189-90.

## Chapter 11

1. Amy Sherman, *Kingdom Calling: Vocational Stewardship for the Common Good* (Downers Grove, Ill.: InterVarsity Press, 2011), 67, 70-71.

2. Miroslav Volf, *A Public Faith: How Followers of Christ Should Serve the Common Good* (Grand Rapids: Brazos Press, 2011), 31-32.

## Chapter 12

1. Barbara Brown Taylor, *The Practice of Saying No* (New York: HarperOne ebook, 2012), 5.

2. Ibid., 10-11.

## Chapter 13

1. Sherman, *Kingdom Calling*, 59-62.

2. Richard Bauckham, Matthew 25:14-30 in *The Lectionary Commentary: Theological Exegesis for Sunday's Texts*, edited by Roger Van Harn (Grand Rapids: William B. Eerdmans, 2001), 149.

## Chapter 14

1. Witherington, *Work*, 67.
2. Wright, *Challenge of Jesus*, 186.

## Chapter 15

1. Andy Johnson, *1 & 2 Thessalonians: Two Horizons New Testament Commentary* (Grand Rapids: Eerdmans, Due out in 2014).
2. Ibid.
3. Ibid.
4. Ibid.
5. Ibid.
6. Ibid.

## Chapter 16

1. For a much fuller explanation, see my book *Answers for Chicken Little: A No-Nonsense Look at the Book of Revelation* (Kansas City: Beacon Hill Press of Kansas City, 2005).
2. Andy Crouch, *Culture Making: Recovering Our Creative Calling* (Downers Grove, Ill.: InterVarsity Press, 2008), 170.

# FIND **FREEDOM** IN THE **COMMANDMENTS**

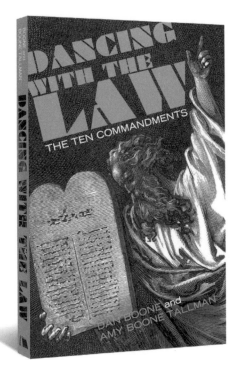

In *Dancing with the Law*, authors Dan Boone and Amy Boone Tallman challenge us to—like the ancient people of God who revered and celebrated law—look at law as a sacred gift that points the way to the life God intended for us. Through this earnest exploration of the Ten Commandments, they offer us a new perspective on law—one that makes us dance with freedom, liberty, and the gift of life.

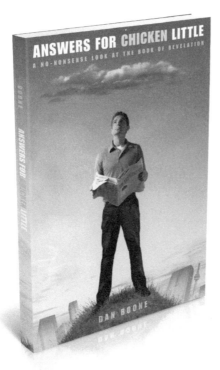